T0131498

THE RIPPLE EFFECT OF BEING

A Thought Experiment

C M H Hill

BALBOA.
PRESS

A DIVISION OF HAY HOUSE

Balboa Press books may be ordered through booksellers or by contacting:

Balboa Press
A Division of Hay House
1663 Liberty Drive
Bloomington, IN 47403
www.balboapress.com.au
1 (877) 407-4847

Because of the dynamic nature of the Internet, any web addresses or links contained in this book may have changed since publication and may no longer be valid. The views expressed in this work are solely those of the author and do not necessarily reflect the views of the publisher, and the publisher hereby disclaims any responsibility for them.

The author of this book does not dispense medical advice or prescribe the use of any technique as a form of treatment for physical, emotional, or medical problems without the advice of a physician, either directly or indirectly. The intent of the author is only to offer information of a general nature to help you in your quest for emotional and spiritual well-being. In the event you use any of the information in this book for yourself, which is your constitutional right, the author and the publisher assume no responsibility for your actions.

Any people depicted in stock imagery provided by Getty Images are models, and such images are being used for illustrative purposes only.
Certain stock imagery © Getty Images.

Print information available on the last page.

ISBN: 978-1-5043-1713-9 (sc)
ISBN: 978-1-5043-1712-2 (e)

Balboa Press rev. date: 03/20/2019

DEDICATED TO
JEN BURDEN

1932-2016

May only that which is for my Highest Good
pass through my electromagnetic bubble;
all else to be reflected back
with benign intent.

May only that which is for the Highest Good of Others
pass out of my bubble,
all else to be reflected back
for contemplation.

Contents

Acknowledgements

I am grateful for assistance from many people in the course of writing this book.

I thank my friend Jen whose innate kindness and wisdom amazed me, and her sense of fun and curiosity sparked me on an amazing journey of discovery of the unexplainable. I still see her eyes smile and feel the warmth of her words "How Marvellous!" Thanks also to my friend Toni Pallesche who challenged my spirit to take responsibility and gave me faith, my friends Tony Putnam and Andrew Tilley who engaged me in caring conversation with cups of tea for the soul, my friend Tia Johns who reflects me and helps me laugh and cry, my friend Rachel Evans for describing the doorway to the joy of music through her patient and kind lessons, my friend Suravi Anand for allowing me to tag along as she delights in life, my friend Solange Ingabire for inspiring me to look forward as well as back, and to love the moment. My friend Johanna Kijas, who patiently and wisely listened and reflected my development over half a century has my gratitude and lifelong affection.

I am grateful to PollyAnne Hill for her genuine encouragement, and for providing an inspiring space to write and be. Feedback has been enthusiastically and generously offered by Rochelle Carrig, Sophie Kijas, Darrell McCarthy and many others - including random strangers - who have discussed concepts in answer to my questions with concern, contemplation and often, delight. In particular, I thank Joanna Fay for editing this book.

I thank with deep gratitude the people who have helped me look within, and I honour the experiences of this fascinating journey of life. I thank those who have loved me. The Ripple Effect of unconditional love provides energy for both creation and resilience.

I thank with awe the help received from my publishing consultants Al Sampson and Gemma Ramos at Balboa Press.

Finally, I wish to thank Julie Lewin for providing the spark for this book.

Introduction

This book has grown from a series of personal experiences over the last few years which could be described by most people as unusual. Some of these experiences have been included as background to the development of ideas. Whether you believe my stories or treat them as fiction is irrelevant to the essence of the book. The experiences encouraged me to think about how we interact and react to events both internally and externally. There are billions of stories of the ripples we create in our time/space dimension. No story is more or less important than any other.

This is just one story of mine, about how I started to see, question and then understand the colours of souls.

In the 1990's I was a single parent running my own business and had commenced a PhD. I contracted glandular fever and consequently developed Post Infective Fatigue Syndrome (PIFS, also known as CFS or ME). My eldest daughter became sick at the same time. She was thirteen, and although she is extremely intelligent, she was physically unable to complete high school. We were both confined to bed for two years. The effect of this disease is not like the ripples of a pebble in a pond, but more like having a boulder chucked unexpectedly into a small puddle. I have felt like the puddle trapped under a rock for the last couple of decades, annihilated by the effects of a boulder of a microscopic "bug".

The virus which caused our lives to suddenly stop was Epstein-Barr. EBV is unpleasant, but only devastating if you happen to meet a number of criteria, including (it is believed) being the unlucky recipient of one "faulty" gene. When activated, the virus permanently changes the chemical make-up of the physical body, as if there is a sudden and catastrophic climate change, or perhaps as if an atom bomb has gone off inside. The fall-out continues for years. It feels like a once fertile rain forest has been denuded by acid rain, or a glitch in the central processing unit has reconfigured the energy systems and the computer has crashed.

The feelings I experienced were similar to the feelings anyone going through a life changing traumatic event experiences, but I did not understand the pattern. I just wanted my previous life back - to be cured. However, my altered immune system meant I developed several auto-immune conditions and contracted other viruses, relapsing for months at a time. I also developed migraines which were accompanied by visual disturbances, including seeing "auras" around people.

When this happened, I was fascinated. The auras were different, but some seemed to convey characteristics which reflected abilities and interests, as if we each have our own identifying Soul Colour/ personality structure. I wondered if the migraines I had viewed as further problems were actually gifts, providing a different perspective, like a window to information we cannot usually see.

One incident was significantly different. I attended a talk by a "disciple" of Amma - the Mother who Hugs - and when he walked into the room he seemed to me to be cloaked in blue, with a white light shining around his head. It struck me that this light apparition was similar to paintings and stained glass window depictions of Mother Mary, and I wondered if artists over the last thousand years used those colours to convey that the mother of Jesus was the "carrier" of the message of peace and goodwill for humanity.

I felt like the colours around people had a language I did not understand, as if the colours contained information ready to be communicated. Most of us cannot normally see auras, but perhaps we feel them subtly, like we feel a soft breeze on our face but cannot see it.

I began to wonder if the different colours of our auras reflected our individual thought patterns, or if we think differently because we see the world through the colour of our own aura. I wondered how thoughts were formed - how our thoughts could evoke emotions, and how our feelings are expressed physically. I wondered if physical pain, memories or an emotion - like joy - has recognisable colours or if luminosity - when someone's face lights up - makes their colour sparkle.

If auras reflect thought, I wondered if thinking in a particular way would help me get better. I had read many books on positive thinking - but the virus still lived inside me and thinking positively did not seem to change that anymore than positive thinking will grow back a lost limb. The colours I could see seemed to indicate there was more to us than positive or negative thinking.

I started to closely observe how people interact, reflect off each other, diminish or enrich the lives of those around them with their words and actions. I realised how obviously thoughts can be reflected in micro expressions and movements even when people concentrate on being polite. Whenever we interact, there is refraction and reflection, rippling from one person to another. I could see energy entwine or clash, meld or deflect, depending on the pattern of communication or relationships.

On occasion, I could even see anger lash out like a dragon, searing those it was aimed at, or leaking out of the person who was angry like smoke from a dragon's nostrils.

Those times during which auric colours were visible to me felt strange - as if I was given a tiny glimpse into a different dimension. I could see how our energy surrounds us and ripples around others, lighting them up or dampening them as if there is a natural resonance effect of being with other people. I wondered why we interact in the ways we do - if the colour of us responds to the colours of others, or if our colours change depending on who we are with.

Electromagnetically, we can be energised or drained according to the direction of flow of energy. I saw how energy could be generated with intention, and gradually understood we have the ability to find and feel joy whatever our circumstances. But some of us have to work harder, with intention to direct that ability to learn the power of our reactions and responses in each moment.

I wondered if we intentionally delight in the gift we are given as the present, and share that delight would our lives feel better? If understanding how our thought patterns change our external reality could be like stepping into a new dimension? Can we learn to open - or wrap - the past as a present to our future?

Please don't look for answers here, this book is about *questions* we should ask ourselves. Just asking the questions may alter your perspective - perhaps even change your world - not because the questions are profound, but because *your* answers matter. Thinking about your internal response may help you understand the Ripple Effect of your Being: how what see and hear and feel *matters* - and how what we do, and think, and say, affects those around us.

The Ripple Effect of Being infers that our existence affects others. Just by BEING. How we interact with everyone matters, and what we think and do creates the ripples of those interactions.

Just as learning to read opens a dimension enabling knowledge, learning the language of our soul colours may provide a similar quantum jump in wisdom. Then we will, hopefully, understand our responsibility for the Ripple Effect of our Being.

The aim of this book is to provide a platform for thought so we can understand the ripples we create and receive on a level that is not just physical, because what - and how - we think has a Ripple Effect both within and around us. This is important.

At the time of writing, there are two suicides each day in Australia. How many more people are in enough internal pain to attempt - or even think about - the ultimate escape? How we treat each other can have a detrimental, even fatal, effect. Interactions can also be nurturing, life affirming and joyous.

All interactions are complex, and some of those complexities relate to the personalities and egos involved. This book suggests that soul characteristics are involved, and that at the core of our being - our soul, we have a "colour" which in part dictates how we perceive and react to situations.

The colour model is used in this book to assist in understanding the innate traits of people: the colours of our soul, personalities and ego. As each of us is unique, these colour layers may help us understand our strengths and weaknesses, talents, desires and emotions.

The colour model also proposes a paradigm for developing awareness beyond our five senses. We cannot be sure that we see exactly what other people see, but some see more clearly than those of us who need glasses. Some of us have more acute hearing or sense of smell, and we all have individual preferences in taste. Some of us have a more sensitive touch - or are more sensitive to pain. We all have these senses, but our levels of sensitivity vary.

In the same way, our internal sensitivities vary. However, there is little language to describe how we feel internally in situations or interactions, or why some of us are intuitive, or fun-loving, or critical. Just like we can get glasses or hearing aids, perhaps we can develop tools which enable us to learn how to focus better on our internal senses.

All of our senses contribute to our consciousness and we may have more than five senses available for use on a moment to moment basis. Raising our consciousness of our internal makeup can help us ensure that the ripples we create are thoughtful, and genuine reflections of a soul at peace with itself.

The final chapter of this book gives an example of a thought experiment to practice internal dialogue through conscious awareness of the information gained through our senses. This practice is an intentional study of interaction, and will create a difference in your life - if you intentionally practise.

1

Soul Colour

"Thoughts don't become things; thoughts ARE things."
Eric Michael Leventhal

I believe that we are born with natural abilities - innate personalities and individual interests - which are directly related to the colour of our souls. Our soul colour is separate from, but additional to our genetic history and upbringing, as if there is an additional dimension to our lives unrelated to family. Our "soul colour" - the colour of our natural abilities and proclivities - is the colour which provides the key to us, the colour of the window to our perspective on life.

We feel like we live in a three dimensional world, but believe it is the fourth dimension of time. What if we actually live in the fifth dimension, where everything is changing constantly - feeding back on itself, every action, word and thought changes our reality from moment to moment? Fluid rather than physical? An electric universe - colour and motion rather than mass?

Try this as an example: put your phone on camera, and hold it up. You can see the scene in front of you through the screen of the phone. You know the phone still acts as a phone, but at that moment, you can see through it as if the phone has become virtually invisible - it is a just frame for the scene in front of you, to take a snapshot in time.

In that moment in time, I bet you are not thinking about the fact that through the phone you can access all your contact and calendar details phone, skype, email or use social media to contact anyone, anywhere in the world, look at other photos, play music and videos, watch TV and movies, do calculations, use maps and find out information about virtually anything. At that moment, it is just a camera - and usually pointed back at you as a selfie.

Our mobile phones can be likened to our current consciousness, containing our history, the people we pay attention to, our public and secret lives. If our phone is lost or stolen, panic surrounds the loss of our contact numbers, conversations and experiences - of what is "inside" rather than the phone itself.

What if we could see inside ourselves, into the parts of us that are usually invisible? What if we could learn to use all the tools inside us just as we can learn to use all the applications on our phones? We could choose mindfully what we devote our attention to. Become more aware.

Even more interestingly, what if we could take a photo which changes time, or shows the result of a path we didn't take? Or capture a moment in life, and see in slow motion the invisible waves from the choices we made affecting everything? See the ripple effect of that moment going within ourselves, causing reactions and responses on our physical, emotional, intellectual and spiritual levels, and at the same time going outwards, creating reactions in those around us?

What would we choose to do differently, if we could understand how a small action subtly changes us and affects others, rippling through our current and potential relationships?

If we could see clearly how that ripple effect causes changes in our lives, would it change the way we behave on a moment to moment basis? Would we appreciate the impact we make on the world?

Could there be a dimension we live in where every word matters, every action has a reaction, every single thought has a tangible consequence that our three dimensional understanding has failed to recognise? Einsteins' theory of gravitational waves is described as ripples in the fabric of space/time. Perhaps this theory can be applied to our experience as humans with the energy we weave in the fabric of a dimension we cannot physically see. The Ripples of Being. How our soul colours merge to form the tapestry of life.

I had a dream about how energy works. I saw a drop of water bounce into a still pond, and the ripples circling out, joining with ripples from other drops to form networks like a lightning ball, or an electrified spider web around the world, then zooming back in to the original drop. I understood that we only see the ripples on the water, not the ripples through the air as the water drops, or the undercurrents formed as the drop descends through water, continuing its momentum and transferring energy effortlessly into the watery environment, becoming one with it. Creating a difference just by being where it is at any moment in time.

This dream made me wonder if our awareness is sensitive enough to register the way we impact on each other and our environment. If we are aware of ourselves enough. If we understand how we think, what we feel, how experiences affect us, and why we react.

Can we really change our inner worlds, or are there patterns which are lifelong mindsets? Is it possible to become happier just by choosing thoughts, emotions, experience and reactions which give us joy, or does it require something deeper - like an understanding of why we think and feel differently to others?

Many people believe we cannot control our thoughts. This book challenges that belief and provides a thought experiment about the layers within us that colour our thoughts and generate perspectives through our moods. I believe it is possible to become aware of the patterns of our thoughts and reactions, and that we can change how we think by responding with greater awareness of our internal world.

The research for the proposed thought experiment has come from a number of areas ranging from ancient philosophies through studies of Buddhist monks regarding the effect of voice on mood and the environmental effects of meditation, to quantum physics and psychological theories.

I have found my research over the years diverting, confusing and complex, so I have attempted to simplify my understanding into a framework that has provided me with a way to make sense of my world, in the hope that others may find this thought experiment useful. It is not intended (nor does it pretend) to be a scientific, metaphysical, psychological or academically rigorous pursuit, but these disciplines were involved in my search when they became relevant to my journey.

Perhaps the discussions and questions in this book can be best described as psychosophical. Julio Ozan Lavoisier suggests that psychosophy starts where psychology ends - not from what has been revealed, but from what *is revealing* about our inner selves. Psychology can be defined as the science of understanding human mind and behaviour, but pyschosophy is more akin to wisdom of the soul.

Science has provided an enormous amount of information about our physical bodies. We *have* bodies, but we *are* souls, and this psychosophical experiment seeks to engage our inner wisdom.

Individuals in any society come from vastly different experiences, belief systems, family patterns, education levels, personal values, and levels of social engagement. Even if they grow up in the same household, there are individual differences in manner, thought patterns and attitudes that are inexplicable.

Ask any mother - did her babies, her children, behave exactly the same as each other, or do even twins have distinctively individual perceptions, behaviours and progression rates through the "accepted" stages of development? No matter how similar our backgrounds, there will be subtle - or not so subtle - differences in our personal goals, likes and dislikes, beliefs, practices, and patterns of thought and behaviour.

Our genes, apart from being family specific, present us as male or female. This is the first of many distinctions. Finding out the gender of a baby is a defining moment in the life of that child. From the moment of birth our gender defines our social identity, and how people react to us, even before we ourselves have any concept of gender. As we grow, how we are seen through this "skin" of our biological makeup affects how the world treats us.

We cannot choose our gender and although the lines are fast being blurred, we are still treated differently if we are male or female. What we look like impacts on how people react to us. We cannot change our gender, or easily make ourselves taller or shorter, or change our skin colour, body shape or bone structure. Our soul colours, however, have no gender or size, shape or skin. As most people can't see them, there is no prejudice.

Our bodies are like our cars, but our bodies are not us, just the vehicle we get around in. We cannot make a quantum upgrade of our appearance in this lifetime like we can buy a new car, but we can become more aware of our skills as the driver of that car. We can learn to see past our gender, skin colour, size and shape to recognise and value who drives this vehicle - our soul.

How we gain information about each other is discussed in the chapter on our senses. I believe that we receive more information about people than we are consciously aware, and propose that we can "feel" our soul colours, and respond to people on a dimensional level beyond our five senses. Understanding how we do this could be like transitioning from watching black and white television to a full colour 3D experience. The story is the same, but instead of watching, we could feel part of the experience and grow our level of consciousness in a different way.

This book proposes that we experience our lives through our own uniquely coloured glass, as if we are born in a bubble of consciousness that gives us an individual perspective on life. Our perspective is important because it affects not only our lives, but the lives of those around us.

To illustrate this, imagine we have layers of colours. The layers of our colours show us how and why we think and act in the ways we do. How we project our personality, and how we internalise what is projected to us. There are dimensions of ourselves we cannot see, but which have real effects on our lives. The colour model applied to these colour layers of outward personality, inward personality and what I call the ego-dragon will be discussed in chapter five.

Through this model, we can understand our subtle differences by seeing that our soul colours reflect how we harmonise and blend in the big picture. Viewing ourselves and others through this coloured bubble model may help in understanding who we are, what our needs are, and how we prefer to interact with the world as well as identify our innate gifts and abilities.

These colour layers are like the key to our inner BEING - the ripples of energy we emit.

I find it helpful to describe soul colours in terms of the chakras of the body, or colours of the rainbow, or even notes in a scale.

Western civilisation has categorised colour through the rainbow of seven primary colours (ROYGBIV), and music as seven notes (A-G). These categories are simple (but useful) descriptions of the continuous spectrums of colour and sound, but let us begin with an understanding of chakras.

The seven chakras are "wheels" of energy within our bodies. According to Indian philosophy the chakras are the major energy centres of our physical bodies. Chakras can be described as pumping stations for energy, similar to the way our hearts pump blood. Traditionally the chakras are attributed to physical sites aligned with our spine, and described with colours as if our bodies have an internal rainbow reflecting the flow of energy and light: the base chakra is red; the crown, violet. Associated with each chakra is a particular sound as if music is part of the energy.

Yoga is an ancient Indian practice intent on spinning the wheels of each chakra to ensure energy flows freely through the body. Yoga is not a competitive sport - it is a practice designed to look within.

Each pose in yoga is designed to focus on and harmonise an area of the body with mind and spirit. The poses require physical exertion and concentration, giving the opportunity to recognise the areas of flow or blocks in how our body feels. Understanding why some poses are more difficult allows us to see why blocks exist so we can work through the emotions or feelings which come up during the practice of yoga, on a moment to moment basis.

The loop of constant attention required for each pose - noticing, correcting, and physically, mentally and spiritually surrendering, to "become" the pose, provides an energy cycle in preparation for the final phase of meditation when the chakras are aligned. When we feel this level of "bringing peace within", we are (theoretically) able to access Universal Wisdom.

This is not an achievement of one yoga lesson but requires daily practice over many years. Different cultures have practices with similar aims - to find the still, quiet voice within, by working through issues of the body and mind first. Uncovering the essence.

For the sake of this thought experiment, imagine there are natural abilities associated with each chakra colour, and that each of us has a primary, or dominant energy centre which can be referred to as our soul colour. This soul colour reflects the key we play in.

Viewing ourselves as a Being with a primary soul colour provides a paradigm with which to understand how we behave, think, and perceive the world. The qualities inherent in our soul colour may be evident in things we find we are most interested in, our innate skills, what enthrals us when we are "in the moment", being ourselves, or "in the flow". It is the colour of the glass we look through when we are genuinely relaxed, involved and open. Our soul colour may be described as our inner moral compass, our true essence.

No chakra colour is more important than any other. All colours come together to form clear light, and all seven chakras are required to form the complete energy system of our bodies. So there is no hierarchy involved.

A way to explain the metaphor of colour centres I am trying to describe is to think of a house with seven rooms. Each of those rooms has certain characteristics, or functions. Each of us has seven chakras like all the seven coloured rooms, but we are born and live predominantly in one room which is our "home" room, as if we are given the key to our essence. This is the room of our essential, authentic self.

A brief introduction to the characteristics of each of the room colours follows, adapted from Shepherd Goodwin's website[1]. These

---

[1] https://shepherdhoodwin.com/whats-your-role/

descriptions give an insight into the colours. You may recognise characteristics within yourself from several colours - reasons for this will be explained when the layers of colours are explored in chapter five.

RED

People who play in the red key will be most interested in helping or supporting other people. As there is no hierarchy involved in the colour spectrum, there is no hierarchy within a colour either, so nurses, doctors, massage therapists, cleaners and chemists are all likely to be red souls. One of the preferences for the colour red is to work in structured environments, where there are clear objectives and rules to live by. Red souls usually have strong humanitarian ideals, and need to bring comfort to others in some way. Recognition or reward is not sought - being with people and helping them feel better creates a sense of satisfaction and joy. As red is the colour of the base chakra, Red souls provide a link between the physical body and the earth, so there is an innate desire to assist the natural flow of the environment.

ORANGE

A person born into the orange room will be most interested in art, fashion, music or the development of skills and innovation in any area. The orange souls are particularly adept at working with their hands as musicians, artists, or in crafts, assembly, or mechanics. Orange souls have exceptional skill in understanding how things are put together to create efficiency or beauty, but can be seen by others as complex - often difficult to understand, or over-emotional. They may seem unfocused and start many projects but never finish them, but if dedicated and focused, can create a masterpiece of unique brilliance. Orange is the colour of the reproductive energy centre, and provides a link to creation.

YELLOW

Yellow souls love being in groups such as sports, and enjoy physical activity. They are often physically powerful as well as productive, and value loyalty. Strategy and negotiation are fun for those whose soul is composed in the yellow key, and they enjoy adventures, travelling and exploring. The travel industry, the military, or any organisation they can feel part of a group provides happiness. Yellow is the colour of the solar plexus chakra, which is the energetic centre of our bodies.

GREEN

The green key opens the door to interest in everything - philosophy, science, research - and green souls enjoy working in research institutes, universities or information technology. Often seen as detached, green souls are the observers of life, and shine at investigation. The green chakra is the heart chakra - the beat and balance of our lives.

BLUE

People born centred in the blue chakra will love performance arts, stories, comedy, politics, languages and any form of self expression. They desire to share knowledge, perform in public, and usually really like applause. Blues tend to be good at sales, teaching and the performing arts, and are excellent speakers and entertainers. The throat chakra is blue and reflects communication.

INDIGO

An indigo soul filter indicates an interest in metaphysics, spiritual, religious or ethical areas. Indigo souls feel the need to help large groups of people. They value honesty, compassion and experience satisfaction by bringing comfort in a spiritual sense. The third eye, situated in the forehead, is the site for the indigo chakra and is believed to be attached to the pineal gland or "spiritual centre" of the body.

VIOLET

Violet souls make excellent Chairs or Judges. They are more likely to listen intently than talk and have wisdom and integrity in leadership. A person born in this violet bubble will be ultimately, but often quietly, dominant in relationships and usually wield power with careful judgement and responsibility. Joy at soul level is provided by drawing people together to help connect or complete goals. The crown chakra is violet and provides a link to the universal unconscious.

I have also heard the Colour Roles described as:

Red	Keepers of children
Orange	Watchers of the Spirit
Yellow	Defenders of the Flame
Green	Speakers of Knowledge
Blue	High Teachers
Indigo	Seekers of the Spirit
Violet	Healers of the Spirit.

I think these labels are aptly descriptive, but will use chakra colours not only for simplicity, but because there is a synchronicity with colour, vibration and music discussed in later chapters. As a precondition for the thought experiment, let us assume we all have a "true" colour, a natural resonance, a soul colour, which affects the way we see the world as well as how others see us.

I believe our soul colours are evident from birth, but may not establish recognisable patterns until puberty. At school, those choosing to find a quiet corner during lunch to read science are likely to be green souls - those choosing poetry or plays, blue. Blue souls can also be found with orange souls in the backstage of the theatre, practicing lines while trying on costumes being designed, or having their faces painted, by the creative and artistic orange souls. Violet souls may be directing the production, or coaching soccer games on the field - identifying talents in others and encouraging confidence in using them. Yellow souls will more than likely be on the field, kicking or hitting balls, keeping active and developing skills with their body. Indigos are most likely to be singing in choir practice because that is what makes their body feel good, or involved in "deep and meaningful" discussions, and red souls will be happiest being part of a group so they can interact and form connections with other students, which is what resonates and ensures their body feels good.

Our "true colour" may not shine through because we have layers. We play many different roles in our families and communities, and each of these are important. The soul colour is what speaks deep inside when we are loving what we are doing. Bear with me as I attempt to convey some insight into the practical observation of how soul colours are expressed.

Imagine you are at a dinner party with people who all have skills which add to the experience. One person has prepared the house - cleaned, shopped for supplies, organised the night, serves the food, cleans up, ensures everyone is comfortable and provided for (Red). Another cooks the food to exquisite perfection, or arranges the flowers, adds creativity and style, or provides the music and atmosphere and dresses with individual style and elegance (Orange). One will have spent the afternoon playing tennis, and will want dancing or party games to complete the night out (Yellow). Another enjoys the stimulation of intense intellectual discussion (Green). There is also an entertainer - someone who effortlessly talks, tells stories to enthral or create laughter (Blue). And someone who is slightly spooky - insightful or perhaps even uncomfortably able to tap into what you are thinking (Indigo). Another is a natural magnet - everyone likes them, they enjoy being entertained, and can amicably settle arguments if they arise because they seem wise (Violet).

All people at this dinner party are "normal" but very different, and express their individuality in ways that display their natural gifts. A person may be performing a role they have "taken on", but let us assume these dinner guests are operating from their true colour. I have never been to a dinner party with seven guests who epitomise these "soul colours" clearly, and it is unlikely I ever will, but in all the dinners I have attended, I can identify individuals who classically represent each of the colours.

A dinner party can be viewed as a micro-society, but an even distribution of soul colours will not occur in real life dinner parties. Usually, when organising a dinner we will invite "like-minded" people who we like, and who think like us. For example, those with green souls are more likely to have green friends because they are interested in having stimulating discussions with each other, while yellow souls may be part of a sports team who enjoy eating together after a game.

When light is split, colours separate according to their different wavelengths. Similarly, people tend to group together according to their interests and abilities. However, as the bandwidth is different for different colours, violet souls are unlikely to know very many people who also see life through a violet filter. However, in the same way that certain notes in a musical scale will resonate with each other (for example, the fourth and perfect fifth), a Violet soul will naturally enjoy the company of other colours, and in particular, information and energy from green and yellow souls.

This is an example of natural resonances between people. Those who were born in different coloured bubbles from our own may attract us - we immediately "click" and enjoy their company - or we may find there is a level of friction or disharmony which we experience as outright dislike, or vague discomfort. Like the seven notes of a scale, some notes naturally harmonise while others feel discordant. Dissonant notes are seconds, sevenths, augmented fourths and diminished fifths.

It has always fascinated me how harmony or dissonance often happens between strangers. Without much interaction, friendships are formed or no connection is felt - or even instant enmity evolves for no obvious reason. I have found the soul colour model provides an intriguing explanation.

I remember the first time I saw the colours of a musician. I had recently had a virus which affected my vision and sometimes I could see auras around people. It was a gorgeous balmy hot Adelaide night at Womadelaide, and I was standing on the outskirts of small stage set away from the main areas listening to the amazing sound of a Libyan band I had not heard before.

As an encore, Emel Mathlouthi came back on stage solo and started playing her guitar and singing Leonard Cohen's Hallelujah. I saw colours grow around her, blossoming in strength and energy. I may have put it down to lighting effects if I had not felt the air change - the "feeling" of the night. The atmosphere felt charged - electric and emotional.

Suddenly the colours surged out over the audience and I watched in awe as the audience rose, from sitting on the grass to their feet in one movement. I knew they could not see the colours, but they felt them. The experience was magical, and most of the audience cried with emotion. It is the most memorable moment I have of a concert. Looking back, I have felt the same thing in performances many times, but I had just not seen it. To see it, was life changing.

How do I explain that? Is that what the Ripple Effect of Being looks like?

Singers and musicians who connect to energy in that way seem to understand the resonance, rhythm, taste and texture of music. They bring life to the song, and evoke an emotional response in the audience. The emotions evoked are universal - cultural and gender differences seem irrelevant in that moment. It is as if the musician can step into a song-line and take the entire audience with them into that space.

Our reactions to music cannot yet be scientifically explained, but those reactions are real. Music resonates within us, bringing up memories and emotions, invoking a desire for movement and dance, or tears. Music can produce different brain wave patterns and altered states of consciousness. If we could consciously produce energy surges such as the one I witnessed, what would we choose to play?

Our resonance as individuals follows similar patterns to music - genre, rhythm, melody, harmony, beat, accent. We evoke emotions in other people just by being. Is it possible to spread emotions like love, joy, hope and peace, so the people around us feel happier? If we could clearly feel the emotions of those around us, without them having to try to explain with words, would we behave differently toward them?

Can we become aware of our own Ripple Effect of Being? This is the thought experiment journey I began, which I would like to invite you on.

2

The Golden One (TGO)

This is the purpose of the experience - to make us
feel the overpowering presence of a mystery.
CG Jung,
Psychology and the Occult, 1939

This journey evolved over many years, but blossomed in a series of insights. There was a turning point, an "A-ha" moment, but I need to explain the lead up.

One morning I woke up, reached for my computer and googled "medical intuitives". I had been very ill for a long time and was frustrated by my inability to recover from a series of devastating viruses. I do not know why that term came into my mind, or what exactly I was looking for, but I stopped looking after I found Julie and booked a workshop with her.

I learned from this workshop that medical intuitives have perfected the gift of communicating with - seeing, feeling and hearing - the body in a dimension which is different from the physical. They have learned to master the tools of this gift in a way any of us can master tools. Through practice. Coupled with the gift of an innate intuitive soul colour.

We might all be able to learn to use tools to sculpt, but only some of us are able to create an ornate piece of exquisite beauty. Learning how to sculpt from someone who can't use a hammer and chisel is not going to spark a desire to find the "David" in a piece of marble. We all have the ability to learn how to use a hammer and chisel, but it takes talent, skill and a lot of dedicated practice to carve the beauty of a face out of a hunk of stone.

Even if we have an innate gift for something, it can be hard to become skilful and we are unlikely to begin to practise with intent until someone who has mastered the skill can show us how to use the tools. Intuition or connection to the universal unconscious, like any gift or talent, is enhanced with use and practice.

It seems we have a shed full of tools we don't even know the purpose of - let alone how to use them - and they may just be lying around getting full of cobwebs. Perhaps psychosophy is the art of learning to use these tools to define our essence, sculpt the beauty of our souls, draw on our internal wisdom and play our internal song. But how do we do this when we are groping around in dark sheds, unaware of the tools waiting to be used?

There are many paths on the journey to discovery, and no one is the "right" one. We have to find the one that resonates with us. Practicing the skills required for communication between the soul, body and mind might feel like dreadlocks being combed out into soft, silky hair. The knots and tangles come undone as we begin to understand how free we are to move through life in harmony.

My spiritual dreadlocks were hurting when I booked the workshop with Julie in November 2013. I was feeling more than a little uncomfortable, and unsure as to why I was there, or what I could hope to achieve from my compulsion to meet this medical intuitive. I was curious and open - but the workshop took a twist I could not have expected.

Julie was giving me information on the various things she does, and as an aside, her previous experience of channelling came up during our discussion on the first day. She had used her additional skill as a medium to give readings to people, but had become frustrated in these sessions by people wanting to be told by a "higher authority" what to do, rather than looking within themselves and being responsible for their own decisions.

I had read various books about mediums and channelled information over the years. Books such as "Seth Speaks"[2], the Ra Material[3], and "Messages from Michael"[4] had intrigued me, but never prompted a desire to investigate channelling as an activity. The greenness of my soul colour make up meant that I was more interested in the actual information than the process of channelling.

The term "medium" has become popular as a description for people who have the ability to channel - see or hear information not usually accessible to our third dimensional space/time reality. Mediums have recently become a popular television entertainment subject, but cannot be explained scientifically. Channelling is a controversial subject, and it seems I am digressing here, but bear with me.

There was an enormous amount of interest a century ago in the ability of "channels" to access information they could not possibly know. In the last hundred years channelling has been discredited by scientists unable to explain the phenomenon and often dismissive of the claim to be able to "see dead people" or "remote viewing". Fraudulent use of the term for financial gain by people without the gift has not helped.

---

[2] Roberts J "Seth Speaks: The Eternal Validity of the Soul" Amber-Allen Publishing Inc San Rafael 1972
[3] Elkins D, McCarty JA, Ruekert C "The Ra Material: An Ancient Astronaut Speaks (The Law of One) Whitford Press Atglen 1984
[4] Yarbro CQ "Messages from Michael" Berkley Publishing Group USA 1980

Carl Jung's doctoral dissertation (1902) was focused on the phenomena of channelling, and formed the basis of his groundbreaking work on the "collective unconscious". I found this surprising, as I thought he had based his concepts on dreams rather than channelling. Everyone dreams several times each night, and there is no scientific argument that dreams occur. Dreams can be described as "not reality", or as a language our souls use to communicate - but scientifically, dreams also have no adequate explanation.

Channelling is not a part of our daily lives and is not yet accepted by mainstream science. But paranormal abilities have, and continue to be, examined and tested scientifically. Many people think paranormal abilities are just too weird and do not believe they are possible.

Weird it is. And interesting. Julie was dismissive of her ability to channel, and did not see it as useful in the work with which she was currently involved as a medical intuitive. I hoped the ability to communicate beyond our physical reality was a real phenomenon rather than a "sideshow trick", but I had personally never seen anyone channel. My personal soul colours urge me to test and question rather than accept or reject without evidence. So I go places many choose not to.

Having the chance to witness the process of channelling was immediately interesting. I had not, however, considered how people feel when they channel or are involved in a channelling session. I was about to find out.

The following is an excerpt from a transcript of our conversation. I have added commentary, and started with an example of her presentation that first evening.

> *Julie: We are here to have the human experience. You can be an aesthetic and meditate in a cave in the mountains, but when you come out and experience all the human*

emotions and get angry - where is enlightenment in that? Why not be enlightened within the chaos you have to live in?

I still experience fear, anger and sorrow, but I know how to get back to that place where healing is a given, not just a hope.

We talked about her previous experiences with healing work when channelling came up in the conversation. There was a sudden "flash" and the room appeared to glow with a golden light. I was startled, and more than a little curious as we both said "Did you see that?" at the same time. The golden glow continued as we talked, and was unexplainable.

Light has many facets that are not yet understood completely. I believe light can carry information, and when we become aware of changes in the light around us, we can choose to be open to "knowing", and even communicating in ways beyond our verbal and body language.

I had no prior knowledge of Julie's ability and did not expect the workshop to include this phenomena. This event was a small sidetrack at the time, but the information I received later became important. This is a transcript of the event with Julie.

Cathie: How do you channel?

Julie: Nobody showed me how to channel.......Let me think....

At this, the light changed dramatically:

Cathie: Wow.....and the room went normal. How can you not accept this as a gift?

Julie: To do what?

Cathie: Well… you were about to channel (laughter).

Julie: Ok…so I'm about to say my prayer…..OK. Can you see the shifts in my face? ….. Maybe if you ask me a question.

Cathie: Ummm…..Is there somebody here?

Well… give me a break. I had no expectation of this channelling session, and did not have any specific questions I wanted to ask. We discussed channelling, and I encouraged Julie to just let go of her reservations about it and accept the gift.

My curiosity was sparked, and I had a feeling that her ability to channel was connected to her work as a medical intuitive, but I could not have explained how. I was still sceptical, but intrigued by what I had just witnessed. I think I was expecting Julie would be able to contact "dead people", and perhaps hoping my Dad would talk to me through her. Mostly, I wanted to watch, out of curiosity.

Julie: Getting into that space is kind of weird. I feel them here in my throat like a pressure. Now what I'm seeing is a bright light in the room. It's filling my vision. Now it's come down inside my head. Now I feel like I'm melting……I feel like I have melted out through my feet and my hands.

At this stage, the room went golden again. I watched in awe as Julie's body and face were replaced by a series of other very different faces and clothing. I was awestruck and fascinated. And frozen with shock.

It was the moment when reality changed for me. I have since read that according to String Theory, it is possible to access other "dimensions" by changing your vibratory rate. Some people are naturally able to access a dimension the rest of us are unaware exists. But String Theory is still unproven. As is channelling.

But when you see a doorway open into an unproven realm, and a glimpse of the impossible is visible, perceptions and beliefs can change. Forever. I felt completely awed.

Cathie: Wow....Who is here?

TGO: We are The One.....Sometimes known as The Golden One. (TGO)

It has been a long time since we had the opportunity to speak.

I was completely unable to think of anything useful to say or ask. There was a long pause...

Cathie: So, speak.

The glow was still around her, but the faces had disappeared and Julie was obviously in discomfort. She breathed heavily, grimaced, altered her position, and looked in pain. She groaned, while I just sat there dumbstruck, not knowing whether to continue or cut and run. Her face cleared.

TGO: What is your question?

There was unusual static on the tape, for this one session only during the entire three day workshop. I have since learned about the electromagnetic frequencies which can be a sign of the authenticity of this sort of energy work. I will attempt to explain more about that in later chapters. My response is inaudible on the tape, but I think I must have asked about my life purpose, or why they had come.

TGO: To explore what humans call the third eye. You are being shown the process for opening the third eye which can be quite intense for the physical body. It is almost like the birthing canal as a baby is born. The third eye needs to be stretched, physically as well as metaphysically, to allow the vibration to come through.

Cathie: Does the amygdala have a role in this?

I knew about the pineal gland as the likely brain section described as the "third eye", but was curious about whether other parts of the brain were connected or involved. The amygdala is involved in processing emotions - especially fear. Perhaps the question was an unconscious reflection of my own amygdala in overdrive.

TGO: We don't understand that word? Is it part of the human brain?

Cathie: Yes.

I figured a "Golden We" would know everything - the answers AND the questions. But it could be my accent. They seemed to ignore me to get on with their rather gruesome explanation.

TGO: The opening is in the forehead above the eyes and above the nose and it goes deep within like a tunnel and it is like the birthing canal where the cervix dilates. So there is a dilation process which must be endured before the full extent of the opening through the third eye can be experienced fully.

I wondered why would you want to go through a birthing out of your forehead. Vaginal births are bad enough.

Cathie: When the third eye is open, what are humans able to see?

TGO: The universe. The entire universe is open and available in its entirety. Today you spoke about fractals.

> *When the human third eye is opened fully you experience*
> *the full fractal consciousness of the universe from ….*

At this point, the tape Julie gave me of the session cuts out, leaving about 40 minutes completely unplayable. I asked if she had the same problem, but hers played all the way through, so I got another copy of the tape from her. Exactly the same thing happened - the new copy cut out at the same point. She was as confused about that as I was. But I was confused about everything at this point.

From notes written whilst listening to her tape, the rest of the channelling session was a description of the painful contractions involved in the rising kundalini energy and how the pineal gland sprays liquid in the brain to brighten visual perception internally as well as externally. It sounded like a slow and painful process. "They" suggested my life purpose would not become evident until I had done the work required to induce this pineal ejaculation.

Julie and I had not heard of this part of the brain spraying before. Isn't the brain just mushy, and already wet? I researched it, and found that DMT or dimethyltryptamine is sometimes spurted as a sticky substance by the pineal gland.

DMT is an "illegal" psychotropic substance used by shamans to induce spiritual journeys and is known as "the spirit molecule". The pineal gland apparently gives us a dose for free if we go through this long and painful process of forehead birthing - sorry - spiritual awakening. We also get several doses every night during REM sleep, and if we experience severe physical stress. Or a near death experience. Makes you wonder doesn't it?

I was also told during this session that I could become a channel, but that I would have to allow some changes to my voice box for "Them" to use it, and let "Them" take over my body for the channelling. I was repelled by the idea of "allowing Us to step fully into your body", and their sinister "resistance causes discomfort" made me distinctly uncomfortable. I wondered why they seemed to expect I would go through that to get a "next phase" of my purpose. I didn't want a purpose. I just wanted to get better so I could get on with my life. I had no intention of being a channel - it was way too weird.

Although I had practiced yoga in my late twenties, meditation to allow the vibration of light to move through the body, inducing the pineal gland to spray the brain with DMT was new information to me. The technique described by TGO was like a recipe, and I am not good at following recipes.

(As an aside, I learned through practice over the next few years that the space where the vibration and light changes is where "magic" begins. It is as if you can change your brain and find "something else" within. Without drugs, without medication, without expensive courses. Just dedication and practice.)

The channelling session ended when I asked about life on other planets. They left. Suddenly the room changed back to normal, as did Julie's face. I felt frustrated with myself for being inarticulate and not knowing what to ask. Also a little insulted that they didn't give me a definitive answer - like they couldn't be bothered with stupid questions.

As soon as the channelling was over, I started questioning the reality of it. The whole experience had quite scared me. It also crossed my mind that it could be schizophrenia - either Julie or I could have been hallucinating. But schizophrenia is not a joint hallucination.

She could have been making it up. But why? What would be the benefit to her? And how could she have projected light and images in that way when she was not expecting to show me how to channel? Most intriguingly, why did the recordings of the entire three day workshop only have problems during the channelling session?

I know what I saw. And it rattled me, and made me question everything I thought I knew, and was actually very frightened. The thought of them being able to just lob in, as if they were waiting for the "invitation", and were aware of the things Julie and I had discussed that day, I found intrusive. I was also blown away by an entirely "new" possibility, awestruck by an experience I had not expected, and excited. Gobsmacked is probably the most appropriate description.

However, it was not an experience I wanted to repeat. My curiosity was more than satiated with respect to channelling, although my interest in unexplained phenomenon grew, and I occasionally researched these on the internet. I felt uncomfortable and a little panicky when I first started reading, but the more I read, the more I understood the uselessness of fear of things we cannot yet explain. My awe and curiosity over-rode the initial fear.

I could not explain this experience of channelling but it felt significant, so my curiosity was sparked and I started researching metaphysics. I did not become obsessed about this research, but my level of awareness regarding reports of UFO activity and other phenomena such as light orbs and electro-kinesis was raised considerably.

I did, however, become obsessed with the third eye, and began to meditate in a way I had previously considered slightly self indulgent. In my twenties I had meditated as part of yoga for fitness, but certainly not with the intention of creating brain contractions. I had understood the benefit of meditation following directed exercise, and was familiar with visualisation meditations. Concentrating on opening the third eye was a different level entirely.

Over the next year, several things happened which were bizarre and unexplainable. It was a very difficult year, but also enormously exciting and intriguing. I booked Julie for another workshop, but did not really know what I wanted out of it, except that things were moving fast, and mostly, I felt backwards - or at least, at times I was struggling and way out of my depth in my quest for health. In the meantime, I commenced a journey of curiosity that was not related to what I thought I was looking for.

Let me explain how I came to this journey by going back in time a bit.

3

Developing Perspectives

"There is a precise shape of emotion, and a sound
that when played, "creates" that emotion."
Dr Manfred Clynes

A few years ago, I lost my hair - I developed alopecia. It was devastating, even though my hair had never been a source of vanity as it was fine, limp and oily instead of thick, curly and luxuriant. I decided to take the opportunity to buy a series of wigs and have fun with it, rather than stay home and cry.

Within a very short time, I was divorced, retrenched from my job, and had upset my family greatly. I wasn't sure if that was because they did not recognise me, or if they were so upset for my losses they couldn't talk about it.

I found that I was treated completely differently by people depending on which wig I wore. One was like putting on some intellectual-looking glasses, one was like disappearing into the societal veil of invisibility for old women, and one in particular got me a lot of attention, offers of free drinks and smiles from random strangers.

My family and close friends often failed to recognise me until I spoke to them, and even then did a visible double-take resulting in shock and embarrassment. On both sides. It had not occurred to me that I was only me if I was in my own hair, but it was always worse if I took the wig off to show them who I was.

Some people started to avoid me, or would try to make themselves feel less uncomfortable by making jokes about my (lack of) hair. In front of me, or behind my back - I could hear, or feel, the ripples of the laughter. Other people would treat me with careful sympathy, as if I was dying of cancer and needed to be shown I was still valued. Only a few treated me as if I was just me, as if wearing someone else's hair on my head was not the most shocking thing I could have chosen to do, and applauded my bravery. They still have my gratitude and respect.

I have heard it said that courage involves feeling the fear, but doing it anyway. Well, the fear did not go away, but I gradually became less sensitive to how people reacted to me. (Except when the wig fell off unexpectedly, as happened on the odd occasion, causing derision, embarrassment and once, what looked to me like a near heart attack from the unexpected shock).

I'm still not sure why I didn't just stay home and watch television, but I learned more about other people during that time than I had in my life before. I also learned that just the way someone "sees" me creates ripples of emotion within my body. Careless remarks would make my stomach swirl or hurt, my heart pound and my face tighten. If they were jittery, I would become agitated. My nature and upbringing somewhat lacked emotional awareness so this was, for me, a surprising insight - I had not felt so judged before.

At the time, I wondered if our hair has something about it that we don't understand in addition to our obsession with beauty. I wondered if hair somehow reflects personal information in some subtle way, and if wearing someone else's hair confuses the message. My eyes were the same, the way I walked, the clothes I wore were the same, but I was suddenly treated differently in direct response to which wig I was wearing.

I also saw how we don't cope with imperfection in others. I started watching reactions to people with disabilities or obvious differences in appearance. It shocked me.

I saw the same cut off, avoidance and embarrassed discomfort I was sometimes subjected to, in the faces of those who saw strangers on the street who were not "normal". And worse than that, I realised I did it too. This was in the late 1980's, and I believe we were in a more materialistic zone then. Or maybe I was just younger. I'm sure kids still stare and comment.

At the time though, I wondered what had happened in society for people to "slide off" those who are seen as not perfect. Why are people judged on physical appearance, when we have no freedom of choice about that? If we could choose our bodies and faces, would we all choose perfection? What is that anyway?

But back to my story.

After I was retrenched, I got drunk and cried for a while, then got a volunteer job working with children with cerebral palsy. I found I could sometimes "connect" with them, and understand what they were trying to say without the frustration of language boards.

Being stuck in a body which does not respond is mind-blowingly frustrating, and trying to communicate with the rest of us who rely on the spoken word is severely limiting if you are hanging out for a conversation and your mouth will not co-operate. I realised the children I was working with loved that I understood them, but I found the level of concentration required was exhausting. I wonder now if this is the same way animal whisperers communicate, and I was just exhausted because I was trying to learn a new skill.

I started studying a masters degree in business and was attempting to care for my own children to the best of my ability in the midst of the fall out of divorce. I found trying to understand the children I was working with more demanding than understanding a financial statement.

At University the tutorials were interesting, because I was surprised at how case studies involving the same facts and figures could be interpreted so differently by other students. In any class, there were usually only a couple of other people who arrived at similar recommendations to mine.

Obviously, there is no "right" answer in a complex situation, and everyone will give different aspects (manufacturing process, human resources, product development, marketing, finance or economics) a level of priority based on their analysis of the situation and personal understanding of the problem. Whatever the recommendation, there was a perspective each student could add to give an additional depth of insight based on their expertise and values.

Structure, style or strategy can be taught and practiced, but talent cannot, and our talents can be surprisingly varied. Some people are really good at managing other people, some are financial management wonders. In addition, management styles are personal. Some people are consultative and others naturally autocratic but management studies are based on the premise that we can (in theory) become better managers if we understand the complexities involved and strive to emulate the things that work well.

In a way, that is also the premise of this book.

I found most students seemed to interpret case studies according to their innate preferences. The way a person thinks predicts their actions. Some people require a level of stability in their workplace, others need innovation. Some people are highly competitive while others prefer to work in a co-operative environment.

Management theories drive organisational direction, practices and behavioural thought for decades. Business has historically been based on competition and profit rather than wholistic environmental co-operation, and the ripple effect of past management theories still reverberate world wide in organisations.

One of the theories we studied in the 1980s was "The McKinsey Seven S" model: Structure, Style, Strategy, Systems, Skills, Staff and Shared Values, which needed to be "aligned" for the business to be successful. Students seemed to naturally understand one or some of these aspects extremely well, but few could comprehensively draw them together in an elegant analysis.

More than that, their area of interest seemed to be reflected in their behaviour. It has occurred to me that the elements of a cohesive business correspond in some measure to our chakra soul colours. There was a tendency for those who understood Structure to be conservative and organised (red); those whose focus was on Skills were dependent on practice, and also on talent and innovation (orange); the students who enjoyed interacting with people - Staff - also liked group work and games and often turned up to tutorials in squash gear (yellow); the Systems people - well, you know - geeks (green); those interested in Style could talk eloquently and entertainingly (blue); those concerned with Shared Values were .... noticeably absent ...(indigo). This was often the element of the model we all struggled to remember in exams. The Strategists could identify the strong points in all areas and bring them together in a way that worked effectively - they kept harmony and could focus a group on an objective by pinpointing the essence, and persuade the entire class to rethink their arguments to bring things together most successfully (violet).

Our perspectives of situations resulted not only from different experiences, but from different inherent perspectives, and case study recommendations could create quite heated arguments in the tutorials. I wonder now if we were arguing about our own soul colours rather than creating a better organisation through the use of a model. Or perhaps it was the layers of our soul personalities coming into play - more about these later. For the moment, let us explore how soul colours of managers may affect the direction or activities of an organisation.

Imagine an organisation reliant on the skills and vision of the original founder. When that person retires or leaves for another job, the dynamics of the organisation will change. The Ripple Effect created by a new CEO will have an impact on all areas of the organisation.

Let's explore, as a thought experiment, the potential impact of the soul colour of the new CEO (although the experiment can be applied to any group leader). This is a brief generalisation as there are obviously a lot of personality and other issues at play, but bear with me as we look at an overall pattern.

A yellow manager is team oriented, and needs to have a lot of interaction and action. He or she inherently understands group needs, but may focus on the game plan rather than the big picture, and may find plundering and destroying competition more stimulating than maintaining an organisation which functions well in the status quo. A yellow CEO may build the company by acquisition and diversification through skilful negotiation. However, the organisation may then risk losing the focus of doing what they do well.

Blue souled managers communicate well and can effectively talk their way into the top job, but may become distracted if the work itself does not resonate with their own goals, and may divert organisational activity to more closely align with personal agendas. As blue souls can be persuasive and charismatic, customers and employees will probably like the person even if they do not necessarily agree with them - and arguing with a blue is pretty challenging.

Red souled people like to feel their life purpose is achieved through their work, are often happy in the doing of the job as an end in itself. They will naturally strive to satisfy customer needs, so customers will be happy and feel well taken care of. Red CEO's can focus on detail or the bottom line to the extent that they may lose sight of the big picture, especially if changing market trends are not analysed with the help of the skills of other soul colours. Getting advice is not a problem for reds, as they like to work collaboratively for the good of the customers, employees and organisation. They like structure, are adaptable to market needs and enjoy doing the job well.

A Violet CEO will have a comprehensive overview of the organisation and an integrated understanding of how functions meld together to create a sum that is greater than the parts. Judgement is usually sound and fair, and decisions are quick, but expectations of others may be quite high, as the violet CEO will challenge each employee to do their best. Customers should find service impeccable, the organisation will be cohesive, and employees should feel well looked after - if they give 100%.

Orange souls like to be technically competent, prefer their job to offer a degree of creativity with the opportunity for mastery of skills, and usually work more effectively if autonomous. They are generally sociable, but operate on different "levels", so may seem frustratingly vague to others, and change direction on a seeming whim. They enjoy providing an endless source of new ideas, and this could result from being in tune with sophisticated market needs analysis - or could be driven by the need for a personal masterpiece. An orange CEO will be innovative, and likely to be at the forefront of new technology - which means an increase in risk, but with big pay-offs if successful. Customers who like to be ahead of the pack will be enthusiastic, employees will be challenged to keep up, and investors should not be risk averse.

Green coloured souls need to be intellectually stimulated to be happy in any job and may need a quiet, personally conducive environment and space to think. A green CEO will usually be concerned about equality, may have a tendency to intellectualise any situation, and will analyse facts and data thoroughly before any decision is taken. Customers and shareholders are generally satisfied and employees feel they are treated fairly, although they may not understand everything the green CEO talks about.

Indigo souls do not often find their calling involves managing organisations, although when they do, their insight and vision can be invaluable. However, they may expect others in the organisation to "intuit" their role rather than providing explicit direction. An indigo CEO prefers to work with a competent and honest support team. The emphasis is likely to be on an integrated market and co-operation rather than competition. Profit sharing for employees or not for profit provision of services to the community are their preferred models for business.

The point I am trying to make is that any colour may provide an excellent outcome for the organisation, but each style is significantly different. Each of these individual CEOs will provide a Ripple Effect within the organisation as a whole. You may recognise a general pattern of behaviour of your boss or spouse or parent in the above colours, or you may see your own preferred work pattern reflected.

There are predictable consequences of our soul colours which create reconfigurations of the dynamics of the organisation. This model can also be useful to understand how people operate in relationships, families, organisations and societies in our daily lives.

Our soul essence colours our perception of the world around us and therefore creates a Ripple Effect throughout our environment. The colour of our soul indicates the likelihood of a preferred pattern of thought and behaviour. Individual differences exist of course, as no-one thinks or behaves exactly like another person, but this model provides a template for understanding preferred types of behaviour.

Actual behaviour is always the responsibility of the individual. No matter what our soul colour, we can choose the polarity of the Ripple Effect we have on others. As Scott Adams[5] said: "Remember there's no such thing as a small act of kindness. Every act creates a ripple with no logical end."

The soul colour pattern described above is a simplistic model, but useful as a starting point. We are not just one soul colour - we have layers of colours. We all have our own beliefs, values, expectations, codes of conduct, ambitions and desires which are unique.

These individual patterns affect how we internalise our experiences and express ourselves to the world, and also affect how we interact with other people. When the essential "us" is not valued by others or masked by us, we can become depressed or experience an existential crisis.

According to the results of a longitudinal study by Harvard University, close personal relationships are the most important predictors of happiness and longevity. The study found that career success, financial success - and surprisingly - health, were virtually irrelevant to happiness. The best indicator of happiness relied on the ability of an individual to form and maintain close relationships, and the level they reported of feeling loved.

Surely then, it is vitally important to understand ourselves so we can form relationships with people who will harmonise with us, and

---

[5] https://awakenthegreatnesswithin.com/40-inspirational-quotes-on-kindness/

honour our true colours. Love us for who we are - just for BEING us. Perhaps it is not the relationship itself which makes us happy, but being recognised by another as unique and loveable despite our faults.

Relationships are not just with significant others, they are internally and externally complex - extending to everyone we interact with. So even if you practice this thought experiment just for your own benefit, I believe you will notice a difference in your relationships. The wider ranging positive result of the Ripple Effect of Being is that your own inner harmony will impact on every person you meet, talk with or even think about.

Understanding the colours within ourselves is, I believe, a step toward understanding how directing our own energy colour can make us feel happy or depressed. Understanding how our colours influence our thinking can also help us become aware of how our thoughts are constructed. When we understand why we think the way we do, our conscious awareness can take a quantum leap.

Thoughts are tangible as energy. We can feel if someone judges us - admires or despises us. Without them saying anything, we somehow absorb the feeling of their intention toward us. Scientists have known for decades that the energy of thought can be measured, but this fact has only recently been possible to explain through theories of quantum physics.

Niels Bohr[6] said "If quantum mechanics hasn't profoundly shocked you, you haven't understood it yet. Everything we call real is made of things that cannot be regarded as real." Thoughts are real, and the intention behind each thought is important.

Einstein's theory of $E=mc^2$ includes mass and the speed of light as inherent in energy. We now understand that energy does not require

---

[6] http://newstoryhub.com/2015/01/nothing-is-solid-everything-is-energy-scientists-explain-the-world-of-quantum-physics/

mass, and that it is possible to move faster than the speed of light. John Archibald Wheeler[7] has gone further, and claims the physical world is made up of information, with energy and matter as incidentals. Thoughts are excellent examples of mass-less, faster than light energy.

The energy of thought is more powerful than we can perhaps understand. We consciously transmit information just by thinking about someone. If that person is receptive, they will feel it on some level. We are like radio transmitters - we can receive and transmit thoughts. Some of us are more sensitive than others.

Thoughts can also project us into the past or future emotionally, if not physically. How awesome is that? We can emotionally time-travel inside ourselves. We can create a new direction for our future by thinking through the plan to get there, or we can vividly remember an experience from decades ago - get lost in thought for a moment as we see, taste, smell, hear or feel a past experience.

Do we think in words or are thoughts a universal language? Words have a vibration behind them which surpasses the language itself. If there is genuine emotion behind a word, you can feel an impact in your body. Kind words make you feel warm and loved, angry words invoke fear. Interestingly, the words can be exactly the same.

Think about how you would feel if the words "Did you do that?" are said with love and gratitude - or with intent to punish. The feelings evoked within the person who hears the words are polar opposites - warm, secure and blessed or paralysing cold terror. As if words are empty shells unless they contain the energy of conscious thought or intention.

Even without words, we transmit information - our mood, emotional state, gender and even educational level may be inferred through the

---

[7] https://www.scientificamerican.com/article/information-in-the-holo graphic-univ/

sound of our voices. The inflexion, timing, pitch and pronunciation meld with the timbre and tone to produce a voice that is unique to each person. Accents identifying the country of birth or major geographical influence when learning to speak are evident even into old age, despite living in other countries or learning other languages.

A person's voice is as individual as their fingerprint or DNA. In the same way, our soul colours are embedded as part of us - recognisable as a pattern, but also unique.

There are physical feelings associated with different emotions which change the vibration of our voices in predictable patterns. Becoming conscious of this effect within yourself can assist in learning the language of your own body.

Eckhardt Tolle teaches that we must notice what happens in our bodies when emotions are stirred in order to reach awareness. Tolle suggests that we must fully feel our emotions to track down the root cause of our reactions. There is a deep wisdom inherent in emotion that speaks to us on a personal level.

Emotions could well be messages to our consciousness from our soul, and perhaps it is our responsibility to pay attention, interpret and then respond. We can then make a conscious choice to resolve - or amplify - the emotions which emerge in every moment. I wonder if it is when we ignore these signals that we end up confused or unhappy or depressed.

What we feel emotionally affects our behaviour. What we think affects our emotions. Which makes me wonder how thought and emotion come together as consciousness. Scientists and philosophers have been attempting to explain consciousness probably for as long as we have been thinking. Our theories still fall short. Interestingly, scientists don't study souls.

I wonder if it is possible to develop a basic philosophy of consciousness not from the platform of a scientific theory, but just from awareness of our own bodies? The functioning of a body is as complex as the universe, and our understanding of ourselves as conscious beings is limited. The scientific focus on the physical functions within our bodies has not greatly increased our understanding of feelings and emotions - let alone consciousness.

Which led me to wonder whether awareness is developed purely through our five senses. Is something missing in our understanding - is there a link to thought and emotion we have not fully explored, which could explain how the Ripple Effect of our Being-ness works?

This chapter has given examples of how the colour of our soul may influence our behaviour and inner thought processes. These patterns will be expanded over the next few chapters, to explore the complexities of people and interactions. The next chapter proposes two additional senses. I believe including these as sensory information available to all of us will increase our understanding of how we perceive, react to, respond and reflect each other.

4

The Seven Senses

"Honesty is the first chapter in the book of wisdom"
Thomas Jefferson

I have always been intrigued about how other people perceive the world around us. As a child, I wondered if the colours I saw were the same as my twin sister saw. I also wondered if we heard things differently because my head pounded in noisy environments, but she did not seem to notice. I wondered how some people could smell - or not smell - aromas, and I also became aware that people have their own unique scent.

I found a person's smell was overlaid by what they did - such as working with wool or horses, cleaning with bleach, gardening, cooking, smoking, or what they ate and drank. Coffee breath was different to tea breath. Alcohol and garlic were distinctive, long lasting smells emanating from the skin as well as the breath.

I observed a layer of scent which was identifiable and uniquely individual, which followed each person around leaving a faint trail in the air. Dogs can smell this for hours, but for me it was fleeting.

One of the things people grieving the loss of a loved one cling to, are the clothes that still contain this unique fragrance of the person.

I also wondered if people felt things on the inside as tangibly as I did. I had a lot of trouble swallowing food I did not like the texture or taste of, my stomach jumped if I was frightened, swirled if I was upset and my throat seemed to close over if I had to talk to people. I did not understand why I was shy when my sister was the opposite even though we were brought up the same. I was seldom separated from my twin sister, so I did not often have to talk - she would answer for me. I was, however, sometimes confused as to why she didn't say what I was thinking when I usually knew what she thought. I was also confused that people did not seem to hear my thoughts.

It was brought to my attention that this was not normal when I was about thirteen. It was the day after my twin sister had a sleepover at a friend's house without me, for the first time. I was sitting in the study with my parents, and I got up and walked to the phone, before it rang.

I knew it was my sister on the other end of the telephone line, but I could not explain how I knew. I remember my mother seemed bewildered that I knew the phone would ring. My father - also a twin - quietly said that it happens all the time with him and his twin, but I realised that it is not "normal" to have a mental connection or to read minds, and I started to close down a sense which until then, I had accepted. I started questioning and discounting it. More than that, I realised later that people don't like the thought of someone able to access their minds - it is a bit spooky. Invasive even. People like to have their thoughts secret. Especially if they are doing something wrong.

Intuition is, I propose, one of our senses similar to smell or hearing, but it has not been completely recognised - perhaps because there is no obvious organ to associate it with such as a nose, eyes or ears. Also, it seems not everyone accepts it as real - even though I often hear people answer the phone with the phrase: "Hi! I was just thinking of you!"

I believe this "sixth sense" of intuition is becoming accepted by society and that there is a swing back to belief in the family member who is "fey". Mediums who talk to the dead, or dream the past or future are starting to have a voice through movies and television shows. Those who have occasional experiences have a paradigm for comparison, but I wonder if there is a seventh sense as well.

My pondering expanded following my next workshop with Julie. I had often re-read the transcript of the channelling session in my previous workshop with Julie (see chapter two), but found it difficult to process. I was confused, and quite frightened by what I both saw and felt during the session, and, never particularly good at communicating under pressure, was rendered virtually speechless at the time. I had little on which to frame any understanding of what had happened. I had no wish to repeat the channelling session, but had vaguely wondered about it in the intervening year - was it spirits, aliens, ghosts, or perhaps even Julie's past lives I "saw".

What frightened me most was that whoever "They" were, appeared to take over her body. Her face changed completely, and she appeared to be wearing different clothes. The "presences" were imposingly calm, seemingly of good intention toward me personally, apparently wise (although a little repetitive and unresponsive to some questions) and for some reason predominantly male, or at least not distinctively female.

The night before my second workshop, I had a strong feeling that Julie and I needed to revisit the channelling. She had not been enthusiastic about my request in 2013, and I was not sure she would want to try it again, but I felt it was important. Julie was ambivalent about my request, but happy to try again.

I particularly wanted personal information to assist my understanding of my life journey. I felt there were some important questions I could ask based on my research and thinking and my conversations with Julie over the previous twelve months. I was not prepared for what actually took place. I asked what "The Golden One" was:

> TGO: We are looking for a way to describe to you... The best way is to understand: The ocean on earth - there is no fragment of water - it is all one. It is difficult to explain.
>
> We are the Oneness, collectively. We are like the voice of the ocean where all is conscious as one - where there is no separation from that oneness and (we) dissolve with the integration with the oneness. ... Does this answer your question?

Well, no, actually. It was a little beyond what I had asked. Try again...

> TGO: We are Vibration - there is no image to go with what we are, from the human perspective. We are from higher consciousness.
>
> Cathie: Are you who we are working toward being?
>
> TGO: We are who you return to.
>
> Cathie: And there are already humans who have returned to that state, that vibration?
>
> TGO: As the soul grows, the vibration is raised until ultimately the vibration is that with the Oneness and the Greatness of simply being Vibration.

That didn't answer my question. I was getting fidgety.

Cathie: And that is part of the Great Plan that you were talking about last time?

TGO: Yes.

Cathie: Can you explain what you meant when you said the "Great Plan".

TGO: The mystery of the Great Plan is in the knowing that the vortex of wisdom is available to all behind the curtain of consciousness. The great awakening is available to all and this time is coming, as the collective consciousness of human beings on the earth is raised.

I had never heard of a vortex of wisdom. I wonder if it is the opposite of the dark vortex of emotional turmoil. I knew about that, but they were losing me over the Great Plan.

The integration of the vibration comes about through practice and understanding Self and the role you play in the Grand Scheme which is part of the Great Plan. For that which is Vibration to expand and be greater than before, the confines that have been perceived need to be removed, so that Consciousness becomes the focus, not materialistic physical expansion.

The Grand Plan is the expansion of Vibration and its place in Consciousness itself.

By this time, I was getting frustrated with the apparent bureaucracy of these plans and the convoluted way they were repeating themselves without the clarity I desired. I thought "consciousness" was being open and aware, not a curtain hiding a wisdom vortex. I was also a little awestruck that the information seemed way beyond my expectations, and truth to tell, disappointed I was not going to hear about ME.

Cathie: These confines that have been perceived, are they the confines of time and space?

TGO: They are the confines of society's evolution and perception of who the human being is really - and this perception is inaccurate, in the perception of the many or the multitude. It is the task of the few to educate the multitude in a way that awakens them to their inherent greatness beyond the physical experience, yet integrate this greatness into the physical experience. In this integration, the expansion of the vibration of consciousness is escalated.

You ask about in "time and space". In words, it is difficult to describe this time and space - it rather needs to be thought - received and transmitted - prior to verbal translation. What is Time and Space? Inter-dimensionally, the concept is not relevant.

At this point I was just confused. Stumped and struggling. They went on:

The work of the few will create a ripple of awareness and awakening around the globe that you will not witness with your eyes only. That ripple will be vibrational and transformational and will elevate the thoughts and perceptions of many in positions where their vibration will then affect the thoughts and vibration of many.

Of course I had the panicky thought that they were alien invaders trying to infiltrate our minds, and Julie and I were being used as stooges for that end. I had not heard about people channelling the Universal Consciousness, and was suspicious and scared. I stopped thinking about questions and tried to listen intently.

The few are like the facets on a diamond and the few will resonate each facet of this message in a different way so that all elements of that transformation will be received by those who have undertaken the vibrational preparation required for this expansion of light into the entire universe.

The journey is the awakening and a natural phenomenon and expected as part of the new human condition.

I couldn't help wondering if this "new human condition" was one of slave zombies for alien invaders.

As the old paradigm falls away, the new paradigm will be the new normal. As souls collectively, instinctively, intuitively, raise their awareness that they are simply vibration and an instrument of the source vibration, and the closer they align or tune themselves to the source vibration, the more expansion is available for the Great Plan to be executed and manifested at a higher vibration.

This was different. As this paragraph was spoken, I could "see" what was being said:

Cathie: So we are music?

TGO: That is an exquisite term to use, to describe the truth of the human condition. The truth, to describe the soul within the human condition. And when one hears the music they are, the body vibrates in resonance to the greater consciousness. That is how transformation can be truly effected globally, quickly and intrinsically pure, without interference of the ego.

I was distracted by conspiracy theories running rife in my head. I was feeling both prickly and uncomfortable. I was also extremely interested. I wondered about the styles of music and particularly popular music, and how most of the songs are about love and the pain of lost love.

> *Cathie: How is the worldwide music industry contributing to, or hindering this progression?*

> *TGO: The music industry in the world is endeavouring to bring into the physical that which is intrinsic in each human being. The human being then stops their search for their inner resonance because they feel that the outer music is all there is, and they don't understand when we say the music is IN you. They think that is for them to bring something out into the outer world. It is not. It is to feel the resonance of every cell vibrating to your unique sound.*

This "conversation" had taken half an hour - channelling can be a slow process. My mind was reeling, and I felt tired from the intense level of concentration required. I also felt awe and surprise at how the session had taken a very unexpected turn.

The whole experience felt very real to me, but at the same time, seemed - from my conservative business background - utterly ludicrous. Julie accepted it nonchalantly, but did not seem to remember what was said - although I felt she also had been "given" some visuals as she received the words one at a time.

I felt agitated, like some mistake had been made. I was on a quest of my own, not a mission to save humanity. I wanted no part in this, and I was feeling way out of my depth. I was admonishing myself that my curiosity had once again led me to bite off much more than I could chew.

I wanted both to rewind the session - start over again, along the lines of my previous expectations - and accept it, embrace the rare opportunity of asking the multitude of questions that bubbled up. I chose to chase the rabbit down the hole.

I had been having dreams about music being coloured spheres, so I asked about the dreams in relation to their reference to resonance of every cell, vibration and the music within us:

> *TGO: We need to go back. Your spherical note. What you are seeing is one point on the vibration in a magnified way. If you can imagine a song of all of those points connected, from a distance you will see <u>that</u> is what makes up the vibration of a song.*
>
> *When you witness one point it appears as a sphere, but when you witness a song it appears as the vibration which can also be described as a rhythm made up of many one points.*
>
> *So, you have a term: one pointed contemplation. What you are witnessing as the song or the note, as a sphere, can be equated to one pointed contemplation as you are witnessing one point in the vibration of the song.*

The term "one-pointed contemplation" was not familiar to me, but I had read about the quandary of quantum physics - that there is an argument about particles or waves, and how both can be seen to exist, depending on what you look for, so I was intrigued.

I asked about how information is received and how - or if - we can tell when it is true. I had read about people who could discern the truth by the vibrations of the words on a page, those who could identify lies by the micro-expressions on the face of the liar, and that attempts by scientists to develop machines to detect lies through measuring heart rate and skin moisture levels are not always totally accurate.

I thought about how victims of crime would be spared the trauma of long court cases if judges were able to "know" the truth. Underlying all that, I wanted to know if the information channelled in the sessions and the visuals I seemed to be shown were true.

Despite my natural skepticism, I felt deep inside my gut the importance of the information.

> TGO: Ultimately the human being will not need to read, auditorily (sic) listen or visually watch, to receive information. When their resonance is attuned or aligned to the source they will have access to all wisdom, all knowing, and the world will become quieter externally.

> As there will be no need for words, which make communication cumbersome, wisdom will be delivered directly through the resonance. As that resonance becomes the communication tool, as people raise their consciousness, they will know their inner song or their vibration so well that doubt, as you call it, will no longer be a phenomenon of the human condition.

> Cathie: So confusion will not exist?

> TGO: That is correct.

> Cathie: And wars will not be possible?

> TGO: That is correct.

We may, one day, no longer need defence personnel or weapons. The money spent on these features of distrust and deceit could be streamed into free education and food security for all. Imagine that.

Cathie: So the question that comes to me is: how do we reduce the friction between people, and the potential for war, quickly and effectively?

TGO: The secret to this if you want to call it that, is for people en-masse to become aware of the existence of the song within them and its rightful role in this extraordinary paradigm shift that has begun: the resonance of the song as it gains momentum and becomes an orchestra of individual songs creating harmony - exquisite harmony that impacts universally and is instrumental in the great expansion of the Great Plan.

And in so doing, people will become aware they are part of the ocean of consciousness and not an individual song.

Cathie: Is the friction between people caused by the fact that the disharmonies are due to not being in the right place or with the right people?

TGO: Friction is because these people are asleep to their song or vibration within the Greater Consciousness.

It is as we discussed before. The music makers create the music, and so people think that is all they need, so they are hearing the songs of the strong transmitters, and believing that is their song too.

And that search within for that inner resonance is being over-ridden by strongly transmitted resonance - often of ignorance, and misunderstanding the true potential or role of the inner song, and how the collective, or orchestra of songs, is the purpose and requirement for the expansion of Consciousness.

It can't be that easy? Awareness of internal identity will resolve the vast problems suffered by humanity?

Then I thought about the hours - and years - of dedicated practice and encouragement required for children in a school band to progress to the level of a world class symphony. Even with the best intention, few members of a school band could hope to achieve that level. But we don't even practice hearing our internal song - it is like we have an instrument we have not learned to play.

I asked how people become aware of their inner song.

> TGO: Through the demonstration of you, meaning each and every one who resonates wholly with their inner song. And being the illustration and illumination of that resonance in physical form. Almost like the phenomenon of a virus. As the virus connects with the cell, it infiltrates the cell, which connects with the next cell, which infiltrates the next cell - this is a good illustration or example of how this understanding of the relationship between the inner song and the greater consciousness will ripple and touch the lives of many, in its purity.

> Each one is responsible for the resonance within their song, and for understanding how this - or that - place in the ocean of oneness at the same time, as the song feels unique and individual. When one has the perception of the oneness, they lose the inner conflict of duality. That is what you describe as unconditional love.

> We are trying to provide a process or description with the least filters - but to describe that which is indescribable and must be experienced as a knowing, for the truth to be understood.

Truth can never be denounced or denied. That is what this time is for, to reveal the inner connection, inner resonance, inner song, the return of the vibration, connectivity with the source that is unseen, unheard, unspoken. It is only known. It cannot be taught, it can only be located through the spark that is triggered like the virus.

This is one virus we would be happy to discover is contagious.

Cathie: *Can it be formulated that way, these sparks? You said it cannot be taught. There must be some way of knowing how to download knowledge.*

TGO: *There must be a strong desire within the individual to tap into the Greater Consciousness for truth and the betterment not only of this planet, but the entire Universe. To tap into the Greater Consciousness for anything else will not create or provide the outcome desired.*

Cathie: *So intention is important in outcomes?*

TGO: *Yes, vitally.*

Cathie: *I have been struggling with the concept of human sensory perceptions. It is generally acknowledged or believed that there are five senses. I am wondering if there are seven and that Intention and Intuition are the two senses missing.*

TGO: *Correct. We are witnessing a rainbow of acknowledgement which has seven colours.*

Cathie: *And I have been trying to link the seven colours with the senses and to the skills inherent in humans. Is this part of the teaching which will help people understand their inner journey?*

TGO: *Correct*

Julie and I were a little overwhelmed by this session. We went for a walk, and then spent the rest of the day discussing previous experiences and trying to integrate the information.

Of course, integrating this amount of information has taken time. There was a lot more to follow over the next few months. In between our channelling sessions, I started researching how the concept of five senses originated, and whether they were connected to our understanding of consciousness.

If our senses are the vehicles through which we receive information - are in fact the platform that enable us to make "sense" of information - I wonder how our senses create or contribute to our consciousness. Most of us go through life unaware of the majority of noise, smells or environment around us because our brains do not seem able to cope with the amount of information available, so we are aware only of that to which we pay attention.

How are our senses even developed? I decided to research what is meant by our senses. Hyper-vigilance - acute awareness of our environment through our senses - can be developed, but requires years of intentional practice, and is not a normal requirement unless we are in constant danger. This is the stuff of warriors or zen masters, not something most of us have to worry about.

The five senses were accepted as the absolute number of senses in the Middle Ages, but before that, internal and external senses were defined in Judeo-Arabic philosophy. The external senses included sight, hearing and smell, the internal senses included taste and touch. Our senses obtain information about our environment, but we can also <u>transmit</u> information through touch, expression, voice and behaviour.

We also transmit information by creating things that other people can see, hear, smell, taste and touch. However, most information we exchange on a daily basis is transmitted through language, which is not a sense. There are other obvious gaps...

Voice, memory, imagination, dreams, thoughts, perception, judgment, intuition, knowledge, intention and attention have not historically been included as senses. But these are parts of our being, without which we would find communication and understanding difficult. So what are the defining characteristics of a sense? I couldn't find a definitive answer.

Since the Middle Ages, scientists do not seem to have questioned the "five senses" idea much, and nor has the general population, apart from adding the slightly spooky ability to "see dead people" or "know" things we cannot logically know. Many people experience an ability to connect psychically with loved ones regardless of distance, particularly in times of crisis. But we have no way of testing this like we test eyesight.

Animals have the same senses we possess, but many have senses of sight or smell which are beyond the range of human sensory capability. Some animal behaviours display a "knowing" beyond our comprehension, such as the migratory patterns of birds and the way a dog can know its master is on the way home.

Unless we are natural animal whisperers, we cannot converse with animals or understand their language and thoughts, but we can gauge their intentions toward us - it is easy to tell if a cat or dog wants to attack or snuggle. So, communication is possible even if conversation is not, but we do not credit animals - mammals, reptiles, birds, insects or even bacteria - with thought.

Why do we believe animals don't think, that they only operate on something we call instinct? Is this arrogance, or an inability to (yet) scientifically measure thought?

It was said by René Descartes: "I think, therefore I am", but can we say "I smell, therefore I am", or "I have a voice, therefore I am", "I move, therefore I am" - perhaps even "I dream, therefore I am"? What defines this "AM-ness", the state of being?

If it is accepted that we think as a state of being, what exactly is "thought"? Language could be argued to be a platform for thought, but thoughts are not just words - thoughts are attached to images, sounds, feelings, smells and emotions which are not dependent on language. Many thoughts in fact, are unable to be expressed by the limitations that language imposes.

In his book "Understanding Aboriginal Culture", Cyril Havecker[8] explains the "clevermen" he studied were "not directly apprehended by the five ordinary senses upon which the physical scientist relies for all knowledge". The ability to communicate - send and receive information - over long distances through thought, dreams or spirit was accepted in indigenous societies.

According to Havecker, Aboriginal people living in their tribal lands were well known for their extra-sensory perception and abilities of the mind. Aboriginal people have, for tens of thousands of years, been able to communicate across vast distances by "tuning in" to a certain vibration or wavelength of thought. Havecker notes that how this is done is still a mystery.

We can see ears, noses, eyes, the tongue and skin. What do we have that "senses" intuition? Buddhists accept the pineal gland is the "third eye", but we can't see it as an obvious organ. Receivers for the accepted

---

[8] Havecker C "Understanding Aboriginal Culture" Cosmos Periodicals Pty Ltd Sydney 1987

five senses are obvious, but if you look at each organ further, hearing requires a complex network of tiny bones, fluid and membranes for resonance, reflection and amplification of sound waves which are then interpreted by specific areas of the brain. We can't see any of these organs, only the outside ear.

We may hear someone talk, but we cannot always interpret it correctly, and it takes years to understand any language eloquently. A sentence spoken with a different tone or emphasis can be interpreted very differently. The ability to speak, to be vocal, is one of the most important attributes of being functional in current society. To communicate effectively through spoken (and written) language requires years of practice. Not understanding a language is like missing one of our senses.

In addition to mastering a language, modulation of voice is an important way we project ourselves, transmit our needs and express our thoughts. There are voice schools so actors can learn to pinpoint the vibrations of vocal emotions. But we are not usually taught how to intuit how other people feel emotionally - we have to learn that for ourselves. We "know" if someone is welcoming or hostile even if we cannot understand what they say, but I wonder how ofter we fail to understand not just language, but the actual feelings conveyed by a voice.

Tom Lubbock[9], before he died of a brain tumour (glioblastoma) wrote:

> *"I think that loss of speech, and of understanding of speech ... these losses will amount to the loss of my mind. I know what this feels like and it has no insides, no internal echo. Mind means talking to oneself. There wouldn't be any secret mind surviving in me. ....*

---

[9] https://www.theguardian.com/books/2010/nov/07/tom-lubbock-brain-tumour-language

> *The mystery of summoning of words. Where are they in the mind, in the brain? They appear to be an agency from nowhere. They come from unknown darkness. From a place we don't normally think about."*

This darkness may perhaps also describe our ignorance about what constitutes consciousness. Being able to communicate with others is essential for social functioning, but we are not traditionally encouraged to communicate with ourselves, to find our "internal echo". This internal echo may be the sum of our sensory information - our personal databank from which we interpret information.

Words can be confusing or misinterpreted even at an elegant level of understanding any language. However, even when you do not understand the language of another person, you can still see their movement, hear the intonation of the voice, see the manner with which they behave, and feel the intention behind their attitude toward you.

If we visit a foreign country and cannot speak the language, it is sometimes extremely difficult to convey our basic needs, let alone have a stimulating conversation. I was in Italy recently with friends and we attended a dinner in the mountains at the house of a woman who is deaf and unable to speak.

I couldn't speak Italian, so I was not engaged in the conversations going on in the room, and I was amusing myself by taking photos. The woman showed me that she didn't have a nice photo of herself for her mantlepiece and "asked" if I would take one for her. I took several which I showed her, and she picked her favourite so I could get it printed.

When I gave the photo to her daughter to pass on for me when I left for Australia, she asked why I had framed a photo of her mother. When I replied that she had asked me for it, she looked blankly at me and said: "How could she ask for it? She can't speak, and you can't speak Italian anyway."

I wonder if someone who has never heard Italian but lives in that culture thinks in Italian? How do we think if we don't have language? Our reliance on language has perhaps limited our understanding of communication in general. But we communicate in many ways that are universal.

I believe that intuition, the sixth sense, enables communication through our thought processes somehow. I tried to research how that might happen.

The pineal gland contains crystals which react to vibration in a similar way to the structure of the ear, except that these crystals are piezoelectric. Piezoelectricity means electricity resulting from pressure, and apparently verbal anger is enough pressure. These crystals can generate electricity if you yell at them - even if they are in a petri dish, not in your living, responding, wet brain.

If we have crystals in an organ deep in our brains that generate electricity when we are suddenly yelled at - we are going to be given a shock. As if our "feelings get hurt", for real. The electrical energy generated by these crystals may even be explained as a vibrational substance of feeling.

The crystals are called Rochelle Salt and since the discovery of the compound by the Curie brothers they have been used in diverse practical applications, such as the production and detection of sound, generation of high voltages, transmission of voice via radio, and to provide the spark in cigarette and stovetop lighters.

One of the unique characteristics of the piezoelectric effect is that it is reversible, meaning that the direct piezoelectric effect - the generation of electricity when stress is applied also implies stress is generated when an electric field is applied. I wonder how that pans out in our brains which are essentially electrical impulse generators?

Our bones also have the property of piezoelectricity, so we feel things in our bodies in ways we have yet to understand. The saying "I feel it in my bones" suddenly has more credibility, and for me raises the question of why our most solid bone structure - our skulls - are like a satellite dish pointing in, towards the pineal gland.

Understanding how this works could be a step toward understanding how emotions are generated, and how we are affected when feeling stressed. The amount and structure of Rochelle Salt, which apparently can form as sand, scale or defined crystals in the pineal gland, affects our level of personal sensitivity.

This difference could explain why some people are inherently compassionate and instinctively comfort someone who is hurting, while others are virtually unaffected by witnessing pain. If someone is overly sensitive to the emotions of others, we even tell them to "toughen up".

We treat athletes with respect because they have developed a genetically superior muscular structure to a level of performance which outstrips the vast majority. We recognise the talent, commitment and practice required to compete in games for our entertainment. Such athletes are singing their inner song - and likely centred in the yellow chakra, doing what makes their being resonate with joy.

For those who resonate in the indigo chakra where the pineal gland is seated, the spooky abilities we cannot yet explain and their skills in hearing and seeing what others cannot are just as valuable and worthy of respect. But I'm pretty sure they don't get encouragement or awards.

Instead, we use television to assault and insult the pineal gland with constant noise, violent programs and mind-dumbing commercials.

As Bill Hicks[10] said, "Watching television is like taking black spray paint to your third eye."

If being yelled at, or watching an act of violence creates a "shock" of electricity, then is there a different vibration created when we send love? This question was a sort of turning point for me in understanding the physical impact of thoughts and words.

How is our brain affected when we yell at ourselves for stupidity, or calm ourselves with loving, compassionate thoughts? Can thinking something have a measurable impact on our physical bodies and if so, can we learn to *think* kindly? Perhaps we can utilise this piezoelectrical system instead of using drugs and alcohol to self-soothe?

To test this out, I practiced changing the way my body felt, just by eliminating destructive self-talk and critical thoughts about others. When I was with people, I noticed more the patterns of their speech and attitude, and found calmer, kinder people were easier to be around. As I got better at catching my thoughts, I found I had to avoid television, the internet and radios because they hijacked my attention.

My head began pounding with excess noise as it had when I was a child. But my body felt lighter, looser, and meditation was easier and joyful.

Meditation is taught as an effective way of relieving stress, but fifty years ago it was viewed by western culture as something "weird" done by Hindus and Buddhists. Ancient practices are the result of understanding and knowledge built up over thousands of years because they produce tangible benefits if treated with the same dedication as athletic practice.

What if such practice builds the "muscles" of the chakras in our heads? The indigo and violet chakras, if honed, could enable or

[10] https://www.brainyquote.com/quotes/bill_hicks_384098

enhance reception of knowledge from the world around us. If we got a feeling that the plane we were about to get on was going to crash, would we listen it? Some people have listened, and survived. Just as interestingly, why do some of us NOT get these feelings? Is it because we have shut down some level of our conscious awareness? Or not learned to develop our innate abilities?

Is the ability to perceive intention, know the thoughts of others, or dream the future an enhanced ability of those with indigo or violet souls, in the same way that orange souls are inherently creative and green souls naturally curious? Do we all have these abilities, but most of us have never attempted to develop them because we are not naturally "talented" so we have no idea how to take the first chip out of the marble to create David?

We are all innately creative and inquisitive. We don't have to be maestros or professors, we can all learn to play an instrument, to paint and to read. Encouragement to develop abilities associated with intuition or intention are not on our radar, so perhaps our general lack of talent in these areas is only due to lack of education and practice. We cannot use a tool we don't know exists.

If we accept that the pineal gland is the source of intuition - our sixth sense, what is the organ responsible for the reception or transmission of intention - our possible seventh sense?

I was fascinated to read about the "discovery" of "mirror neurons" within our brains. They were discovered quite recently by a scientist who ate his lunch in front of a "wired up" monkey and noticed the instrumentation showed brainwave patterns associated with the monkey eating - even though it was just watching him eat.

When we watch something, our brain reacts as if our body is acting it out. Movements of others are reflected by these mirror neurons in our brains, everything we watch is internalised and felt within our bodies, as if we are actually performing the action. This is how we learn to walk - learn anything that requires specific movements.

Mirror neurons are essential for imitation learning. Watching any action will help you learn how to do it as these neurons are involved in establishing memory and recognising patterns of behaviour. If someone falls and gets hurt, everyone who sees the fall will feel it to some degree in their own body. Watching someone dance beautifully is mesmerising because you can feel the perfection on a cellular level.

The mirror cells in our brains reflect throughout our bodies everything we see without us moving, just as in our dreams we can vividly feel as if we are actively involved even though our bodies are immobile with sleep paralysis.

Think about it the next time you watch a murder, theft or violence on a television show, or the pain and suffering endlessly documented by news journalists. Think about the ways we allow the media to use what Marilyn Schlitz calls "weapons of mass distraction". Think about how you are impacted the next time you sit mindlessly through a series of commercials.

Advertisers know that whenever you are hungry - physically or emotionally - their junk food commercial will emerge in your memory as if you are already eating, and as you head for the phone or the car to feed your craving, you may even find their jingle humming away in your head.

There are some very interesting key findings within the research conducted into mirror neurons so far. The neurons receive and interpret facial expressions, which enables socialisation by feeling internally the emotions associated with micro-expressions. Understanding through feeling what is seen provides the observer with a real experiential comprehension of the action.

Mirror neurons seem also to be linked to memory. In fact, mirror neurons spark in response to thought as well as sight - when we just *think* of something that makes us feel good, angry, or physically ill.

What I found particularly interesting is that our internal response to any action is greater if we love the person doing the action. Emotion amplifies the actual feeling in the body from watching the action. Watching a football game if we don't like footy is an entirely different experience from watching the same game and loving it.

This is not about our attitude, but about acknowledging how our inner resonance affects our perception. We have believed that we understand things by thinking about them, whereas mirror neurons show that we can understand the external world because it feels like it actually happens, inside us. Through the filter of our personal feelings.

This is a Ripple Effect.

I wonder what would happen in the world if we learned how to develop these reflections to deeply understand what goes on around us? Are we damaging ourselves by not being totally conscious of the impact of what we see? We are becoming more aware of the way food impacts our internal health, but are we aware that whatever we see - and hear - has an effect within us as well?

Are we damaging our bodies by thinking about pain or disease or things that make us angry? Dwelling on upsetting interactions or replaying arguments in our heads may be rattling these mirrors and filling us with negative resonance. Every thought could affect every cell in our bodies.

We can only know the world through our own bodies. Our sensory organs are our only avenue to consciousness. I wonder if we have not yet fully understood consciousness because we have not been aware of two vital sensory organs - the pineal gland and mirror neurons - providing us with the senses of intuition and intention.

Sense	Receptor
Smell	Nose
Taste	Tongue
Touch/Feeling	Skin/Bones/Nerves
Sight	Eyes
Hearing	Ears
Intuition	Pineal Gland
Intention	Mirror Neurons

It is interesting to note that the only one of these receivers that is not specifically just in our satellite shaped skulls is skin and bones, but the nerves connect these organs to the brain. It is also interesting that there are connections between the senses which enhance them - if we can see something, we hear it better, and if we smell something, taste is more accurate.

Whenever we interact with another person, the seven sensory impacts come into play - we can feel responses in our own bodies. We use language to describe our reactions: "I feel it in my gut", "It doesn't smell right" or "I see what you mean", but the ability to describe the feelings evoked by our senses through language is limited.

Our senses form the resonance of our physical, emotional and mental vibrations, creating platforms for our memories and future responses. The only way we can consciously "make sense" of what we receive is through our interpretation of that reception. As we are each unique, it can take practice to accurately decipher the messages we receive internally. Learning to pay attention and understand what the feelings within our bodies mean is like learning a new language.

We can learn to recognise the signs or symptoms of information such as pain, anxiety or depression and notice the circumstances that trigger the information flow. Having a skilled teacher is always helpful, but this internal language can be very personal and is likely linked to individual memories, dreams and emotions.

From toddlerhood we are taught to control our reactions, and as we grow up we learn to ignore signals such as pain. Some of us don't really understand what the feelings and emotions actually mean and it is easier to conceal them with pain killers than to listen. Feelings exist to give us information about ourselves at a deeper level. By examining this information, we can choose to respond in the moment with integrity.

As our bodies are both receivers and transmitters of information, we project our thoughts and intentions as well and once we understand how we affect other people through our projections, and how our internal self-talk affects our own bodies, we have a responsibility to ensure that we are mindful. Much has been written about mindfully responding rather than reacting to our feelings. Mindfulness can be difficult to put into practice even though the concept is quite simple.

In essence, it is the process of learning to utilise the sixth and seventh senses. We don't have to practice using our senses - how to smell or hear or see - but we can become more aware through paying attention to these inputs by scanning the environment or focusing. This awareness is a skill. The more aware we are, the greater the probability of a comprehensive and integrated understanding of what is going on around us.

Reactions are largely unconscious, and can be vital in times of danger. When we are not in danger we are more likely to respond from reasoned choice. We can choose our words, our tone of voice, our movements *and* our thoughts in line with our inner song. Our senses provide the information for the lyrics, based on our perception of what is within and around us.

I believe that practicing awareness of sensory information impacts directly on our consciousness. When we understand what makes us uncomfortable, we can choose to channel our energy into the thoughts and actions which result in feelings of harmony. We create our own reality by being aware of how we feel inside, and how we affect others.

We make a difference by the things we say and do, and perhaps more importantly, the things we think, but do not say or do. For example, being angry with someone but pretending to approve of their actions will create discord within our physical body as well as our mind and spirit.

Martin Seligman[11], in his book "Learned Optimism: How to Change Your Mind and Your Life" suggests that optimism or pessimism is reflected in our speech - the patterns we use, the words we use. Seligman has proven that optimism is a major factor in our health and happiness.

I believe it has a Ripple Effect on the health and happiness of those we come into contact with every moment of every day. But I also believe that we internalise and project these patterns through the filters of our soul colours. What if, by understanding our soul colour, we can understand more about how we talk to ourselves and view others, and from that understanding, learn patterns of thought and speech to become more optimistic?

This chapter has sought to explain the senses we use to receive and transmit information and proposed that understanding our perceptions and how we interpret information through our individual soul colours is a platform for conscious thought and awareness. This information is building to a simple thought experiment, but first we need to understand the filters we have.

---

[11] Seligman MEP "Learned Optimism: How to Change Your Mind and Your Life" Random House Australia 2011

5

Dimensions of Colour

I didn't really choose my beliefs: I discover I have them
Halligen

In the first chapter, I proposed the thought experiment of viewing ourselves as different coloured "bubbles" of consciousness, and that each soul colour could be associated with predictable skills and abilities or traits. This chapter seeks to delve more deeply into that concept. Perhaps some of you are asking, "Well, what colour is *my* soul?"

Allow me a word of caution - soul colour is a metaphor for use in this thought experiment. The imagery of colour is a model for understanding - a useful tool for conceptualisation. For the moment, let us use this model to imagine that we do indeed have a soul colour which imbues us with certain gifts and challenges.

There are a number of ways to work out which colour most reflects your soul. This is a start:

1. Observe the things that interest you, hold your attention or make you feel good
2. Ask yourself why

3. Ask other people what they see as your main strengths and weaknesses
4. Ask yourself if you agree with their answers and whether your body resonates with their analysis
5. Remember the things you enjoyed doing most as a child
6. Compare those to the things you do now, every day
7. Ask yourself what makes you feel happy

Your answers to these questions will provide some clues about the soul colours described in chapter one.

For example, as a child I loved to climb trees and sit in them quietly on my own, or I would spend hours in the garden watching lizards, spiders and insects. I don't do that so much now, but it gives a clue that I would otherwise have overlooked - that my soul needs quiet time communing with nature to regenerate (high on indigo) and I am innately curious and investigative (high on green). Playing team games was not a favourite past-time of mine as I am not naturally sporty but I am competitive, and I loved to ski and dance (medium on yellow). I did not talk much (low on blue) or consider myself creative or talented artistically (low on orange). I did not need to connect with people, was not neat and tidy or good at developing routine disciplines (low on red) but was often able to integrate information, and could focus with persistence until I understood the wider picture (medium on violet).

So what do these colours mean? My soul colour cannot be several colours can it?

Being high in the characteristics of several colours indicates a matrix of layers. These will be discussed later, but first a brief summary which may be helpful in discerning which colour best describes your inner soul. Some of the information in this chapter is adapted from Shepherd Hoodwin's website on roles and overleaves.

Red: caring

Red souls find joy in helping others, and in organisations that connect them to that purpose.

Orange: creative

Orange souls find joy in artistic or innovative pursuits.

Yellow: active

Exercise gyms are places yellow souls find joy, or any competitive sports, games or organisations.

Green: investigative

Computers and places of learning such as universities or libraries are where joy is found for green souls.

Blue: expressive

Any stage where they can perform or teach is where blue souls find joy.

Indigo: intuitive

Indigo souls find joy in spiritual connection.

Violet: visionary

Violet souls find joy in bringing people together to fulfil their purpose.

Just for interest, red souls come into an understanding of their life purpose before any other colour. Red souls need to work in an area where they feel they are contributing to humanity, the environment or life in some meaningful way, and do not need to go on a quest to complete their life purpose. Even if red souls become ill, differently-abled or are born with a disability, they are still able to effectively fulfil their life purpose.

Orange souls have the ability to create masterpieces in art and crafts very early in their soul development, but are more likely to do this if they team up with another soul colour or mentor who helps them make sense of the information they are receiving. No other soul colour understands how to bring sensory information together in the way orange souls can integrate information simultaneously - this is how an orange artist can produce a painting that "talks". Other soul colours can recognise a work of art, but not emulate the process that brings it to life. Orange souls may get frustrated working with the single-mindedness of green, yellow and violet souls (but often need their intense focus) and are happiest interacting with other orange or blue souls who seem to understand them best, or red and indigo souls.

Having an orange soul does not guarantee excellence in all creative or artistic forms, but will indicate an inherent ability to see things differently and bring them together in a uniquely masterful way. If music is the chosen profession, an orange soul may not become a performer unless there is a colour combination of outward and inward personalities and ego encouraging the dedication for practice with a desire to perform to an audience in addition to that musical talent.

Conversely, a blue soul may have the desire and drive to perform, but frustratingly lacks the inner "spark" for musical mastery or genius. Success can still be achieved as part of a group or through an additional orange soul colour layer.

Green, yellow and violet souls have the ability to concentrate for long periods of time, but need interaction with the other soul colours to gain different perspectives to any challenge.

Some further points of interest about tendencies of groups of colours:

- Yellow, orange and red souls are happier if leadership of a group is good.

- Violet, Indigo and Blue souls have inherent skills involved in understanding the bigger picture.
- Over the last few decades the colour balance has changed as more souls in the blue to violet spectrum have been born. There is a generation of "Blue Rays" and "Indigo Children" who are highly intuitive. This increase in the blue end of the spectrum predicts a swing toward social consciousness and co-operation, and away from competition.
- Soul colour is not dependent on genetics. Although there could be a genetic link to certain talents, soul colour can be completely random in a family.

For example, if a child is born into a predominantly orange or blue family, but happens to be strongly red, there are likely to be challenges for both the child and the family. The family patterns will emphasise artistic projects (which may be left strewn around a chaotic house), constant movement to and from events and even perhaps spontaneous parties until all hours of the night. The child however, will have a deep seated need for order, routine and structured care in a neat and clean environment. Disorder will confuse and frustrate a red soul. Drive them crazy.

Or take the example of an indigo child born into a predominantly yellow family. The child will not be the least interested in playing sport, or even jogging. So the family will be dismissive, or even enraged and embarrassed at the child's incompetence in games, lack of motivation, and desire to be alone in his or her room. The child is also likely to be "sensitive", unable to cope with crowds and loud noises, and may have a tendency to cry a lot when upset. The indigo child will almost always be the one hurt in a ball game if forced to play.

These signals are clear evidence that the soul of that child needs to be respected and nurtured in a different pattern to that which is natural for a yellow parent. Forcing an indigo child into playing sport is simply uncaring. Don't even expect that child to sit on the sidelines and cheer. The whole idea of physical contact sports and competition are anathema to the child, and he or she will find the sheer noise unbearable. Learning respect for a yellow parent's need for action will only come if there is also respect shown for the indigo child's needs.

Families do not behave exclusively according to their predominant soul colour. There are many layers of behaviours and expectations based on a long-standing pattern of history or culture. Often the patterns we learn can be at odds with our own soul colour, and more reflective of the colours of the leading family member or community. This may create internal conflict or a "personality clash" if there is an expectation of conformance, or depression if we find ourselves acting out of character to impress others or "fit in".

Our "personalities" are not our soul colour. On top of the soul colour there are additional colour filters which contribute to our personal signature or vibration. These additional colours are independent of the soul colour. They contribute to how we are seen and see ourselves and how we react when challenged. Sometimes, these inward and outward personalities and egos may cause us to feel at odds with ourselves, as if there are different parts of us vying for attention and wanting different things.

Following is a description of additional colours in our soul make-up.

OUTWARD PERSONALITY

How we express ourselves is part of our outward personality, a filter through which we project our souls to the world. If our bodies are the vehicles in which we travel through life, the outward personality can be likened to the make of that car.

For example, a Volvo may indicate a priority of safety, a Maserati suggests inherent desire for quality and showmanship, and a VW

Campervan could denote self-sufficiency and lack of concern over status. Some outward personalities are flashier than others, but we do not get to choose what our outward personality is, and unlike cars we cannot buy a new one. Any projection of our soul colour is done through this car we were born with.

Our outward personality can assist or hinder us in the achievement of our life goals. The higher the level of fear, stress or misery the more likely our overlay colours will cloud our soul colours like a layer of dust on the car. When we are feeling good about our lives, outward personality shines brighter, and enables greater ease and awareness in our interactions with others.

The premise behind parenting skills and Cognitive Behavioural Therapy is that we can respond more effectively in our interactions with others by learning to become aware of the consequences of how we behave and what others feel about our actions. Being aware of whether our outward personality is sparkling or dusty gives us an opportunity to shake off the dust and interact mindfully.

Table 5.1

Colour	Outward personality	Shiny	Dusty
Red	Restrained	Careful	Guarded
Orange	Attentive	Contemplative	Worried
Yellow	Active	Energetic	Frenetic
Green	Observant	Lucid	Watchful
Blue	Potent	Commanding	Oppressing
Indigo	Enthusiastic	Driven	Obsessed
Violet	Tenacious	Persistent	Obstinant

Our outward personality is often easily recognised by others, and sometimes mistaken as being "who" we are rather than the platform from which we operate - just as we are sometimes judged by the car we drive. Understanding our outward personality is a step toward awareness of how others see us and particularly useful in understanding our own behaviour.

There are subtleties involved in how the shiny or dusty outward personality emanates. For example, a shiny red outward personality means we take care of others, but if we are scared or insulted we put up barriers to ensure we do not get hurt. The consequence of a dusty red will be reduced freedom to explore and experience - for ourselves and those we care for. A violet outward personality can be a non-stoppable dusty bull-dozer, or approaches to challenges in relationships will sparkle with fortitude.

Our outward personalities become obvious in how we project or interact, so understanding our outward personality enables more informed choices. To illustrate how the outward personality appears, let us imagine a scenario where we are faced with a challenge such as termination of a marriage or a long-term partnership.

The break-down of an identifying relationship can be a catalyst for growth or it can blow self-esteem apart. A couple operating authentically from the shiny end of the scale may recognise when a relationship is outgrown, and the breakup will be amicable. However, the anger or grief involved in an unexpected ending of a relationship may push us onto the dusty track for at least some time and to some degree:

A person with the orange outward personality may obsess over keeping their doors and windows double-locked, phobic about the ex-partner violating their home. A person born with a blue potent outward personality could try to control the ex-partner physically, financially or emotionally, and a person with a yellow frenetic bent may become agitated and verbally or physically aggressive. A green outward personality may hire a detective or ask information from friends about the activities of the former partner, while a restrained red may establish strict rules regarding future contact. A violet tenacity may pretend to the world that nothing has happened in the hope that the ex-partner is going through a passing phase and will without doubt return to "normal" - and try to balance life in the meantime. Outward personalities of the indigo colour may seek solace in complete absorption with new hobbies, lovers or spiritual pursuits. These are all normal reactions according to the colour of the outward personality we have been dealt for our lifetime.

The outward personality is the way we express ourselves, how we are seen to act and interact rather than who we are deep inside. Our outward personality can be likened to a shield, and as it is one of our life lessons it can receive a battering. Or create a battering for others.

For example, someone with the orange ability to pay attention may naturally attract a person who has a blue need to be listened to. This can be a relationship with mutual benefit for one who likes to be protected and another who likes to protect. However, a person who appears to be a knight in shining armour at the start of a relationship may end up as our worst nightmare if the expression of these outward personalities is pushed from shiny to dusty. Even if one partner is operating in the shiny end of the scale, the dusty other may make life hell for both.

Although we cannot change our outward personality colour, we can choose to respond from a "positive" expression of that colour (unless our fear is valid and self preservation is at stake). If we are subjected to abuse and ridicule or threat by someone, future interactions with that individual will generally be negatively charged.

Negative charge increases with the level of fear, positive charge increases with love. If we love unconditionally, and know we will be treated with love and respect, we automatically - that is, without thought - act from the positive shiny end of our outward personality.

INWARD PERSONALITY

In addition to soul colour and outward personality colour, we have an inherent inward personality colour. Our inward personality affects our inner reasoning. This is important because the inward personality influences how we talk to ourselves, how our thoughts are coloured.

To use the analogy of the car, inward personality is how we act *inside* the car when no-one else is there: whether we drive carefully or recklessly; keep the interior clean or messy; and whether we are courteous to other drivers or turn into a road rage demon.

It depends a lot on what inward personality we have been born with and the level of stress we operate from, and although we cannot choose our inward personality we can practice choosing courtesy over demonic behaviour, tidy over messy. For example, born skeptical means we cannot change to social, but we can change from being suspicious or paranoid to openly asking questions in search of the truth.

Some of us are blessed with easier inward personalities than others. Despite allegations of "change your attitude, change your life", that change is related to tidy over messy choices only - we cannot change which inward personality we are born with.

The state of our inward personality reflects how we internalise our experiences, and if we are emotionally damaged by someone or emotionally unaware, we slide to the messy end of the scale. Internal resilience is determined by this inward personality.

Table 5.2

Colour	Inward Personality	Tidy	Messy
Red	Composed	Serene	Apathetic
Orange	Skeptical	Investigative	Paranoid
Yellow	Critical	Encouraging	Disparaging
Green	Academic	Practical	Theoretical
Blue	Social	Uniting	Detaching
Indigo	Authentic	Validating	Assuming
Violet	Perceptive	Understanding	Presumptive

It is interesting that being wounded or frightened badly in childhood may create a lifelong predisposition to a messy inward personality. This is a valid human response to abuse (rather than just a "bad attitude"). The effect of the shift is deeper if the damage is inflicted in the formative years of childhood or adolescence, and not mitigated by kindness and unconditional love from someone significant to us.

Feeling loved and accepted provides a platform for resilience. If the love we are given is unconditional, caring and mindful, we are much more likely to be happy and resilient, regardless of what happens to us. Being loved unconditionally enables quantum jumps into the most beneficial effects of the ripples of a "tidy" mind.

Any traumatic experience can throw the inward personality into a spin, and the degree of response is not necessarily directly proportional to the damage caused by the trauma. The following are theoretical examples of how inward personality may be expressed as a consequence of not feeling loved unconditionally - for example, someone subjected to sexual abuse in childhood.

A yellow inward personality will tend to denigrate and even be vitriolic at the automatic level of thought directed inwardly as well as spill over in their thoughts toward other people. Yellow will be a harsh critic, if filled with self hate. A person born with a red composed inward personality is likely to be resigned to the fact that some people do bad things to others, and get on with life. We are the least likely to be affected by abuse - or any form of damage - if we are lucky enough to be born with a stoic red inward personality. This is the most resilient of all inward personalities, regardless of the trauma. Green academic inward personalities, as adults, may become advocates of social justice for victims of pedophilia, but researching rights abuses could become an obsession at the expense of other areas in their lives. An orange inward personality may respond by treating relationships with suspicion, and being unable to trust or accept love. A level of paranoia about protection of children is likely to be evident. A violet inward personality may presume the motives of all people are sexually oriented - which could then affect the integrity of all personal interactions, while a blue social inward personality may start a support group for victims of childhood abuse or find a group for personal catharsis. An indigo inward personality may experience grief profound enough to lose faith in humanity. A loss of connectedness to or belief in the inherent goodness of other people may result in severe depression for young indigos, lasting a lifetime.

These possible reactions illustrate how the hurtful actions of another produce predictable thought patterns in each of the inward personality colours. The thing is, once we understand that we are operating out of a messy interior and understand why, we can cease to be confused and angry, and mindfully choose to stop operating out of fear.

This is important, because recognition of our underlying inward personality can reduce the power of the emotions evoked by the trauma. We cannot change the abuse, but we can learn to respond differently to the pain it caused.

Choosing our thoughts and actions requires dedicated practice, but the outcome is that we no longer react on an unconscious level attached to our memories and thoughts - because we take back the power, and choose to respond authentically to what is happening in the here and now.

Memories which adversely affect our inner thoughts are tied to a negative experience. However, we can learn to change the direction of the energy vortex. We can learn a new internal dialogue based on the intention to recognise the fear, and reject the damaging self-talk.

The polarities of this vortex are simple: fear or love. We do not have to love the perpetrator of the trauma, but we can choose to love ourselves and be kind in our internal reactions to day to day stresses.

Awareness of inward personality operating in the negative vortex may give us a pretty good indication of the thought patterns we cling to unproductively, even if we don't fully understand why our minds got messy in the first place. Ego-dragons are different to our outward and inward personalities - they provide us with an instant indication of our basic fear.

EGO-DRAGONS

In western society, ego is "not a dirty word" and is believed to be essential to success in our world where ambition, accumulation and status are valued. A healthy ego may be an asset, but harbouring a hungry or smoking ego-dragon is dangerous.

Acting or reacting from a flaring ego-dragon creates pain and suffering. The ego-dragon embodies the inhumanity in each of us. Relationship wars are created by rampant ego-dragons.

I believe that the ego-dragon is our greatest teacher, and that being able to recognise the flare of the ego-dragon is a major step toward uncovering our inner song. Our true soul colour cannot shine while we are pampering and feeding pet dragons. Just like the story of the fighting wolves, the good wolf or the bad wolf can win, depending on which one you feed.

Unlike the outward and inward personalities we may have more than one of these dragons. These ego-dragons may operate at the same time, or we can shed them like outgrown snake skins, and take on new ego lessons as our life situation changes over time. Outward and inward personalities are lifelong, but our ego-dragons provide lessons we may transcend with experience, mindfulness and awareness.

Buddhists teach that recognising the role of our egos can enable a shift from ego to spirit and that this is a prerequisite for enlightenment. Followers of Buddhist philosophy consider one hundred and eight "defilements" of ego to be overcome through meditation, mindfulness and practice. This book simplifies the concept of ego to seven categories, following the rainbow model (which may be naive, but is less daunting).

Each of the seven ego-positive and dragon-negative polarities described below have a basic fear and predictable result of the fear controlling our behaviour and thoughts. Resolving the fear will create a positive change in our whole expression of soul colours, as the ego-dragon can hijack our thoughts and actions. However, operating from the positive-ego enables more authentic expression of ourselves through outward personality, inward personality and soul.

When our dragons flare, the root causes of our fear, hurt and resulting anger are divulged. Each time the feelings rise up (and they will be physical as well as emotional), being able to recognise them provides an opportunity to confront the internal dragon.

Fear is ego clinging to the future. Fear shows us how we feel about not "being" enough - that we are not recognised and valued for Being who we are. Anger is the ego-dragon clinging to the past, when we were shown our feelings were not important to someone, and it hurt like hell. All of us have at least one of these basic fears, and just as some inward personalities are easier than others, some ego-dragons are bigger than others.

Table 5.3

Colour	Ego-Positive	Dragon-Negative	Basic Fear	Dragon Flare
Red	Humility	Shame	feeling inadequate	Exhaustion
Orange	Negotiation	Destruction	losing control	Discipline
Yellow	Philanthropic	Hostile	feeling unworthy	Suffering
Green	Willing	Stubborn	change	Avoidance
Blue	Altruistic	Greedy	not having enough	Callousness
Indigo	Dignity	Vanity	feeling judged	Arrogance
Violet	Intrepid	Intolerant	missing out	Impatience

Identifying the ego-dragon within is easy. When faced with a stressful deadline, do you procrastinate (green), set stringent schedules and become extremely disciplined (orange), or perhaps achieve the deadline by working fast, but feel you could have done better (violet)?

We cannot choose to change the colour of our dragons (and again, there may be more than one). If the dragon colour is discordant with our other soul colours, that dragon will make us feel very uncomfortable, and although all dragons can burn, some dragons are more fiery than others.

A note of interest: an orange ego-dragon is more likely than any other ego-colour to consider suicide if undergoing a "dark night of the soul".

Drastic action is unlikely unless the existential fear is sparked and the dragon runs rampant - which damaged dragons under attack do. The ego-dragon is the only soul colour layer that can be life-threatening, but please understand that our soul essence is not ever destroyed, no matter what happens.

We are not taught how to tame or slay dragons, and most of the time they can happily sleep in their cave, oblivious. When fear wakes it however, the searing ego-dragons' breath can burn, send us flying in a flare of internal pain - or desire to inflict pain. Our personalities will be dragged into the dusty/messy zones and our soul colours will cloud over until the storm passes.

When we feel the dragon flare, it is an opportunity to understand - and resolve - our existential fear. This is the dragon we can slay - the only colour bubble around us we can burst. When this happens, and the ego is in the positive end of the spectrum, our soul and personality colours will no longer have the negative drag.

I do not want to gloss over the concept of the ego-dragon, or understate its significance. But it is too complex to cover in this book. This element of our soul colour make-up can create significant challenges in our daily lives - not only for our own moral guidance, but for the feelings it smokes or lashes out in those around us, like an on-going cause and effect experiment.

There are tipping points for these dragons - for some, it may be a small rejection. For others of us, multiple storms can be weathered. But if the winter of our being comes, or the "dark night of the soul", the dragon can slay us. No other part of our soul colour makeup provides this danger.

According to Stanislav Grof, the experience of ego death involves merciless destruction of all previous reference points in the life of the individual. This existential annihilation of the ego is part of the archetypal Hero's Journey requiring a solitary quest into the dark vortex of human emotion.

No-one can undertake this journey for us, but it is not a journey everyone has to go through in each lifetime - it can be seen as a breakthrough point. The journey is one of the hardest faced by humanity, but opens the doorway to the psychosophical - the wisdom of our souls.

When we stop being afraid or angry, our outward personality, inward personality and ego can shine, allowing our unique soul signature to vibrate clear and true, enabling the path of our life purpose. This is the ultimate journey which teaches us how to be responsible for the Ripple Effect of our thoughts and actions, and ensures we are free to sing our own song beautifully.

Even with seven billion people on Earth, no set of soul colours will be identical. Possible combinations of our soul colours layered with outward personality, inward personality and ego- dragons are nearly six hundred and fifty trillion. You may begin to appreciate how we are all individual. These colour combinations are what contribute to the world spectrum of humanity. Of which each individual is an important part of the whole.

As an example of how all the factors come together, I have a friend with a blue inward personality operating out of the positive end of the spectrum, meaning she loves to bring people together as a cohesive group. Her soul colour is yellow - a dynamic, bubbly personality intent on providing experiences with a lot of physical activity and group interaction. She has a red ego in the positive end providing humility, so she is easy to be around, and an indigo outward personality allowing not only enthusiastic dedication to whatever she does, but compassionate insight into those around her. This combination creates a powerful Ripple Effect, and she is great at Being in the moment, and choosing joy. It is like she is a conductor, forming an electrical beacon of intention, and everyone flows around her, in tune. She creates amazing experiences which link her friends together through memories filled with joy: the Ripple Effect of her Being.

Her mother was supportive and loving, giving her the freedom to Be and shine. Not everyone is so lucky. Our personal ambition and desires can be subtly influenced by our family and friends who, although they have our welfare at heart, may have very different soul colours to us. Even if we resonate with similar colours to our family and friends, our personal skill sets and life purpose will be different.

If we feel forced to abandon our own dream to please others, or fulfil roles that are expected of us, there is bound to be a swing at some stage throwing our inward and outward personalities and ego into the negative. Building a life from a platform of negative feelings or dissonant relationships will not promote happiness unless we can understand how to identify and resolve those feelings. These are lessons on the journey of reincarnation.

The concept of living many lives to practice shedding or resolving our fears and needs is daunting - and a little confronting. I asked about it in another channelling session:

> Cathie: Can you explain what we call "reincarnation" please?
>
> TGO: Reincarnation is a word that has been used to describe the longevity of the soul in a way the mind can conceive the possibilities or the potential of the soul.
>
> The soul is an ongoing vibration which continues to grow within the human form, or beyond the human form.
>
> There is a strong desire where souls crave the human experience of emotion, the tactile density of the human

body, the gamut of emotions. Prior to choosing a body to incarnate in, the soul is not concerned - or not affected - by the seemingly negative emotions, nor the seeming positive emotions.

All emotions are an adventure and exciting for the soul to experience. It is when the soul is within the human form they forget their excitement for all emotions.

In choosing the body, they forget their connectivity with the Source. This is when they struggle. The desire to be free of the heaviness overrides the desire of anything else they wanted to experience or explore in the human condition.

However, this is all part of the growth of the soul and the layers or the levels which the soul can embark upon as they travel through the journey of lifetimes in their quest to return simply as light and vibration. Reincarnation is part of the cycle of the soul.

There are specific goals or outcomes which the soul predetermines that they wish to experience in any lifetime. However, that choice is made prior to incarnation and as all souls have experienced, once in the density of the human condition, amnesia occurs in relation to those choices.

Those choices determine the resources required to provide the best opportunity to give the best or closest outcome as requested. It is not only good experiences or good outcomes which a soul chooses.

A soul also wants to test their learning, and asks for situations in the human condition so they can have an *opportunity to draw on their learned resources. Sometimes this occurs, and other times they find it difficult to locate those resources.*

If humans focus on locating their inner song, all their resources are available to draw upon.

Cathie: So going through the "dark night of the soul" is not a bad experience from a soul point of view?

TGO: No. "Dark nights" from a soul point of view is often the very experience they desired. It is an opportunity to locate and use the resources they have gathered through lifetimes and they want the opportunity to make choices that were different with the knowledge and wisdom they have gained throughout lifetimes.

In being able to locate these resources, this is how the soul can progress through the levels.

This information enabled me to relax when I was feeling upset, and to look within so I could determine whether my emotions reflected a dusty or messy personality aspect, a smoking dragon, or a valid moral discomfort with that particular situation. I found (unsurprisingly) that arguing with someone from the smoking, dusty, messy standpoint was a waste of time and likely to end in explosive drama.

Practicing when to stand firm and when to ask forgiveness could take me a while. Psychosophy, huh. Not easy to say, not easy to do.

"Being true" to our soul involves listening to emotions, dreams, and physical feelings. The messages we get from our internal worlds are our own personal challenges to decipher. We can learn our internal language - by paying attention and practicing.

Simple, really.

However, what is simple in theory can be difficult to put into practice. When did we last listen - really listen - to our bodies?

Babies respond in the moment, but learning to develop "appropriate" behaviour from toddlerhood to adulthood may well have disconnected our internal recognition system. Of course, we cannot scream every time we are hungry, and appropriate social behaviour is important, but we are not taught well to listen to our own bodies, or treat these signals with respect. It is like some of us haven't progressed past toddler stages and we are either emotionally incontinent or constipated.

We contribute in a positive way to the world by being the best we can be - without fear. Consciousness in the present is required to recognise the signals which can polarise our lives. Intention predicts how we respond.

Our free will - the way we choose what we think and do - influences the clarity of our colours. Like the weather, we can be cloudy or clear. When we are clear, our relationships are better and our own health is better. When we learn how to shine in our true colours, our energy automatically increases. The energy of those around us will also change. People feel better just being around those who operate in the positive polarities.

I do not mean "being positive" although mindful awareness of how you think is a start. Operating in the positive polarity requires facing our inner fears with courage. That has to start with a deep soul decision.

This decision starts with love.

Love the fact that we are each a unique "song" of colours and patterns, intricately connected with each other. Love the possibility of resonating in harmony with others, and making a difference to the ocean of humanity by being true to our inner soul colour.

Love watching the Ripple Effect of our Being and fully experiencing the vibration of our unique song reflected in the faces and actions and words of those with whom we connect.

When we feel this, we will learn to respect that the chords we play - the notes within us - have a direct impact on ourselves and on others. When we play those chords beautifully, our world changes. We become aware of how we connect through every thought and every response.

This is a lot of information to process in one hit. But you may be beginning to realise that knowing yourself and others is not as easy as identifying the colour of your soul. It is not easy to clarify the layers - it is not easy to change the pull from the dust or mess. It is definitely not easy to face existential fear. And slaying inner dragons may be the most difficult task of your life.

Digging deep into feelings we have learned to ignore can be difficult. Our feelings inform us about ourselves on levels we are not used to thinking about. Taking the next step of changing those things we do which are unconsciously driven by fear can be even more difficult for us.

Don't be tempted to be less than honest with yourself. Keep asking yourself - in every moment - what the emotions you feel are telling you about your soul colour, outward personality, inward personality and the flaring of the ego-dragons. Watch the reflections of yourself, and honestly reflect those around you, with compassion for the fact that every one of us has these layers.

It is a lifelong journey. One of excitement and discovery.

6

Patterns and Reflections

Your every thought is a ghost, dancing.
Promethea

Our reaction to any event is affected by our unique perspective of previous personal experiences which form our memories and beliefs. The way we reflect and internalise any situation is unique - even twins have very different personal experiences, but there are patterns which can be seen to be universal, cultural or familial. These patterns can to some degree shape our habitual responses to situations.

This chapter will explore the patterns we unconsciously cling to. Our family patterns, our cultural and religious patterns and our patterns of thought and behaviour are all important, unless they are not serving us well.

In this chapter I seek to reveal patterns we unconsciously develop within our families and society, and explore reasons for consciously changing our own patterns. I seek to examine how emotions and expectations weave predictable patterns, and the consequences of changing our patterns or having them changed unexpectedly.

A point of interest about cultures: a country can be described by the average soul colour and age of the population. Australia before colonisation was - I venture - an old violet country. Aboriginal people lived in harmony with the earth and other living creatures, including vegetation, rocks, water and the Earth herself. There was no ownership, and teaching and learning was an important part of story-telling. Co-operation rather than competition was a requirement for communal living in the diverse and often harsh conditions.

Aboriginal people understood the "one-ness" of everything and were able to communicate over long distances without technology. Large gatherings of different tribes occurred via "bush-telegraph". People travelled hundreds or even thousands of kilometres to attend important ceremonies or conduct trade. These meetings were co-ordinated through the thought connections of the groups, despite language differences between tribes. There were no written invitations, telephones or internet.

The oral culture provided access to "song-lines" which are as comprehensive as libraries of written information, but exist more like an "i-cloud". The intricacies of the oral historical records were compromised through legislation banning Aboriginal languages to be spoken. I have to wonder whether rampant blue dragons coupled with conquering yellow souls were involved in the "colonisation" of Australia.

Western culture is predominantly at a stage of collective soul development where progress and acquisition is important. As the average soul age of "modern" western civilisation graduates to the next level, we will continue to become more environmentally aware, and more conscious of the damage our need for acquisition has wreaked upon indigenous cultures and their ancient wisdom.

Language - despite the beauty and elegance inherent in any language - falls short of conveying exactly what we feel. Words cannot always adequately express feelings. Not only is our language for emotions limited, but the total effect of emotions on our physical body is little understood.

Sights, smells and sounds - particularly music, can trigger emotions within our bodies - we can suddenly "be" in another time and place as the memory of that smell or song hi-jacks our emotional body. I have seen people taste something, and their eyes go soft and dreamy, their face glows and their body posture alters subtly as they inevitably say something like: "That takes me back …" or "That reminds me of …". How can a forgotten memory suddenly be evoked so vividly? We cannot taste or smell or see or hear what happened in the past. But it feels like we can.

Sometimes the emotions evoked are uncomfortable rather than pleasantly nostalgic. Strong negative physical or emotional reactions can reveal suppressed memories of fear, and it may not be the actual food or music which is remembered with dislike, but the association with the food in a time space which has passed.

Emotions can be likened to the clothes we wear. We can buy clothes with intention, or we can have them handed on to us. We can wear those clothes with pleasure or they may feel uncomfortable. We can follow the fashion, and fill our cupboards with items which become rapidly outdated, or we can carefully choose classic designs with quality workmanship.

The clothes we have in our wardrobes are our history, and some are cherished as "best", some are everyday work attire, some no longer fit but are kept for sentimental reasons, and others are mistakes or even disliked, but we keep them anyway, just in case we need them. They are like protection - an immune system for inclement weather.

Outdated and uncomfortable emotions however, do not protect us - they can make us sick. Just like the clothes we choose, the emotions we choose to keep will hang in our psychic closets even if we are unaware they are no longer needed.

Within our psyche we collect the emotions we have available to call on in an emergency, and these provide our personal patterns of response to any situation. These emotion-clothes are the tools which we have available to use in everyday situations, especially if an event is unexpected or evocative emotionally. If we don't examine the clothes we have available, or we are fearful of throwing them out or replacing them with wiser choices, we may find that our resources are inadequate or inappropriate.

Emotions are as useful to us as our clothes and tell us more about ourselves than we realise. They provide information and protection, and spur us to action - to go to the party in our best dress, to war in combat fatigues, commune with nature in our gardening gear, or retire in pyjamas and dressing gown. When we recognise the emotion we are wearing, we can choose if it serves us well. To do this effectively, we need to learn our personal emotional language.

Edward DeBono in his book the "Six Thinking Hats" helped us become aware that thought has different dimensions which can be directed and expanded. DeBono used coloured hats to signify dimensions of thought. These hats give a platform for investigating different aspects of any problem. The soul colour paradigm proposed in this book provides a similar tool.

The thought experiment in the last chapter of this book proposes developing connections with the seven energy centres within us, and relates them to our soul colour layers. It proposes the centres as coloured mobile phones we can consciously use to "call" when we experience any uncomfortable emotion and ask questions: "Is this my ego hurting? How could my inward personality best address this emotion?". Becoming aware of the source of our feelings can help address them in the moment, with a greater understanding of our personal tapestry, or matrix of colours.

The aim of this thought experiment is to develop an inner language for conscious awareness. Developing an inner dialogue by learning the language of our personal emotions and physical feelings is the first step to recognising our own patterns and understanding our reactions.

It is well known that the emotional state of a person directly impacts on their physical well-being, and that long term emotions such as anger can result in altered immune responses. It therefore makes sense to understand what we feel, so we then have the power to consciously change for our own well-being.

Our favourite places are anticipated with pleasure, and associated with joyful, replenishing experiences. The places in which we experience happy times have "good vibes", and we look forward to returning. If we have a bad experience, the place we were in at that time can appear tainted with our feelings of fear or anger or grief, and if possible we avoid returning.

If we seek out happy emotions by ignoring or avoiding bad feelings we tend not to uncover or address our fear. This means the undercurrent is in danger of emotionally hijacking us at any time, and we spend our energy paddling hard on the surface.

Our patterns can change if we understand why we feel those emotions, view the event from several different perspectives, change the language we use when we describe the event, and choose our thoughts with the intention of being the best we can be. Painful thoughts and emotions can be eased through this process - our response can change our present and future.

Awareness of this process will change the way your body feels, your moods, your interactions and your health. But it takes practice.

When we feel emotional pain and it is not attended to effectively, it escalates in the same way as a broken leg becomes warped or septic if it is not properly set and helped to heal. The "skin" of our emotional body is just as real as our physical skin, and the framework can be broken in the same way our bones break. Broken bones are easy to identify, but learning to identify the source of broken emotions is complex.

If we grow up in an environment of fear, we may not even know what the warm comfortable glow of love and acceptance feels like. The pit of our stomachs may feel like an endless dark vortex we cannot fill. Fear produces adrenaline, and long term drainage of adrenaline energy affects our health on physical, emotional and mental levels.

The English novelist Lisa St Aubinde Teran said "My head was a desolate place and as barren as the bare hills of Le Mache. Until I began to build it, only vultures nested there." Many people live day to day, suffering because they have been hurt and unaware of how to rebuild.

Hurtful exchanges seem to remain as a vibration, a pattern of interaction that repeats. We can find it difficult to forgive or interact in an open and loving way with someone who has hurt us, even if the hurt was unintentional. These patterns become entrenched in our memories, attached to our emotions, colour our perception, and are reflected in the language we use and the way we behave toward that person.

Small, intentional changes can make a big difference to our feelings. Each time a destructive pattern is interrupted, the Ripple Effect is activated. It is possible in this way to build our own consciousness, change our own behaviour, but more difficult to resolve the vibrations of standing patterns because the other people involved may not want to change.

There is an interesting anomaly about the way waves (both sound and water) move and reflect off each other - some waves pass through others, some cancel each other out, and some add to each other to create a sinusoidal or standing wave. Standing waves only occur with certain frequencies, and they favour certain patterns of vibration. The resulting wave is the highest level of vibration with the least energy input.

Perhaps the way we interact can be attributed to the way waves move: we can diminish or feel negated - cancelled out - by a look of disgust or repulsion; pass by people without any interaction or effect on our lives; or be overtaken by a standing wave. A standing wave requires the least energy but can also create the most change.

Resolving discord may not produce perfect harmony, but it will reduce dissonance. With intention, uneasy patterns can be eroded and new patterns built.

I described earlier in this book how intentional use of our seven senses is the "present" we can unwrap. I believe the seventh sense gives us the opportunity to look deeply into the mirrors inside to become aware of the reflections. If we cannot see a pattern we cannot change it.

Buddhists teach the four 'noble truths':

- suffering
- the cause of suffering
- the cessation of suffering, and
- the eight-fold path leading to the cessation of suffering

However, it is interesting that Aboriginal culture has a different focus entirely. According to Kakkib li'Dthia Warrawee'$_a$,[12] Australian Aboriginal people also have four tenets:

- Aildt - accepting that everything is one
- Adtomon - following the path of truth (being true to ourselves and others)
- Dt^{w}ongdtyen - an educative approach that assists in experimental discovery about other people's points of view, and
- Linj - living in the present

These four tenets sound much kinder to me than the Buddhist 'noble truths', because they do not concentrate on suffering as the avenue for learning (not to discount the Buddhist "four pillars" of true work, true play, true study, and true rest). This Aboriginal philosophy feels more optimistic and exciting, with an inherent expectation of joy.

The tenets are applicable irrespective of religion or culture, family patterns or soul colour. It seems we have been learning through suffering for a couple of millennia. Perhaps we could start to learn through joy.

The concept of soul colours provides a model for a range of perspectives which are part of the human experience. As we develop self awareness and our awareness of others grows, we can come to realise the "One-ness" of our Universe, and how our energetic colours merge.

The third tenet described by Warrawee'$_a$ - Dt^{w}ongdtyen - can be learned through practicing the art of "photographing", which is the conscious and deliberate observation of self when any experience is at its height. He suggests it is our own responsibility to educate ourselves through experimentation and reflection to discover emotions and perspective, so we can learn to better understand ourselves as well as those around us.

---

[12] Warrawee'$_a$ Kakkib li'Dthia "There once was a tree called deru" Harper Collins, Melbourne, 2001 3rd Ed

We are our own scientists, discovering what is important right now, in every moment. This is a lifelong education, exploring our true emotions from many points of view. It is also a collaborative learning process because we cannot know how others feel unless we ask them.

The fourth tenet offered for consideration by Warrawee'$_a$ highlights that living in the present is important. Being aware of the reflections that occur in interactions immediately reveals patterns. In every moment. If we intentionally choose to channel these patterns into a positive end of our inward and outward personalities and ego, the Ripple Effect of the past travelling into the future cannot hold the vibration of fear, so the result has to resonate in the band of love and joy.

Perhaps we could all benefit from an educative approach that allows our own experimental discovery in every moment, with the ability to discuss our perspective with those with whom we interact. This cannot happen if we focus on arguing that our perspective is right. Every perspective is valid but is incomplete. It is not the whole truth.

The Ripple Effect of Being, when we have learned to incorporate these four tenets, is a recipe for happiness and harmony. The concept is not hard, but it can be very hard to put into practice, and to practice it in every moment until it becomes part of our Being.

The process of developing awareness can be likened to learning how to dance or play an instrument. Years of mindful practice can result in the exquisite beauty of a performance where every movement of each musician in the orchestra is connected with every movement of each dancer on stage, and with the feelings evoked within each audience member. With dedicated practice and attention we can become aware of our own contribution and ability to flow through our dance of life, in harmony.

Masaru Emoto conducted experiments[13] with water and intention, proving that water responds to thought, sound and prayer, as if there is consciousness within water itself. Crystals formed from the same water but infused with love through directed meditation create different patterns from those infused with the words "I hate you".

I wonder if a sustainable pattern forms in the brains of people we project emotions toward. I wonder what those emotions do to our own wet brains. Perhaps there is a very real physical Ripple Effect of thoughts and emotions we will one day be able to measure.

What sort of legacy do you want to leave behind you on a moment to moment basis? Ripples of anger or Ripples of joy? Only you can change your thoughts. You are responsible for what you say and do, feel *and think*. Even the things that are "invisible" - in your thoughts - are tangible in subtle ways, and have a real impact on your life and on the lives of others.

This is how we feel the Ripple Effect of Being.

---

[13] https://www.youtube.com/watch?v=tAvzsjcBtx8

7

Electricity and Water

Intention + sound = structural change
Masuru Emoto

In the mid 1980's I was hit by lightning. Well, not really hit, although it hurt. More like enveloped briefly.

I was working in the oil and gas industry and lucky to have a manager who insisted that to do my job competently I needed to work with the teams I was recruiting for. Communications, cathodic protection, analysis of pipeline integrity, environmental protection, and safety audit trips were chalked up as I grew to understand the characters of the people who built and maintained the infrastructure for our fossil energy.

My favourite jobs were in the Flinders Ranges. Not just because of the work, or the people - it felt magic being in the landscape. On this particular trip I was working with a cathodic protection technician. I remember the day as being hot, stuffy and grey. We were in a large, flat valley surrounded by mountains when a thunderstorm came in quickly.

Lightning bolts on the mountain tips only just preceded violent cracks of thunder, and I watched enraptured as the lightning spread, surrounding the valley and constantly striking the ancient peaks in a fury I had never before witnessed. It was incredible and I was completely absorbed in watching this three hundred and sixty degree light show.

The air was still, and there was no rain. I remember a strange smell in the air, and the valley took on a blue-grey hue like an old horror movie flashing with lightning. But I became uneasy when I noticed some strange glowing balls in the distance. They seemed to be rolling slowly, and floating above the ground.

They were transparent and looked like electrified blue balls of barbed wire - some of them big as a small house - floating about a metre off the ground, slowly making their ominous way across the flat valley floor. I watched, unbelieving, as they rolled from one side of the valley to the other before they simply disappeared, leaving me confused and slightly anxious, and my ears crackly.

I suggested that we get in the Landrover, but the technician was head-down in the pit, involved in finishing up. I went to the car and stood by the open door wanting to jump inside, but loathe to leave him out there, alone. "Really, I think we should go."

As I was facing him, I did not see the ball come up behind me. But I felt it. Like being hit in the chest with a sledgehammer - back then front - as it passed through me. It was larger than the Landrover but didn't knock me over or burn me - it just kept floating on, passing over the top of him, making his hair stand on end. We packed up and left VERY quickly.

Since then, I have been very respectful of thunderstorms.

Whether ball lightning exists is still a subject of scientific debate. In the '80's I did not have a camera, let alone a mobile phone to film the event, so I cannot prove it. I was interested when I found there were "rural myths" about settlers closing their curtains during storms so "the balls couldn't get in" and the Aboriginal people had knowledge of these balls.

Warrawee'ₐ discusses lightning balls in his book "There once was a tree called deru". His grandfather told him ball lightning crackles and hisses, and has an odd smell. Aboriginal people from his country call ball lighting "Now'dta - just like a little sun". Clevermen of the tribe were said to walk in the clouds and throw lightning balls to frighten wrongdoers. I guess working in the oil and gas industry was not doing good, because it really frightened me.

I am not sure if it is related, but I have had difficulties with electrical equipment, particularly since I developed Post Viral Fatigue. This is not unusual - most people with "chronic fatigue" often have bizarre experiences with electrical circuitry. If someone's car stops, it is usually because they run out of petrol but a person with chronic fatigue will find their car just stops sometimes, as if the electrics are blown. When upset, I have trouble with computers, electric sliding doors, cars (especially electric or computerised), mobile phones, cash registers and lights.

I decided to ask about it.

> *TGO: Electricity is a phenomenon of energy where it is being harnessed to power equipment and lighting. You also are electricity. Your electricity - everyone's electricity - is connected to thoughts and emotions and most people are unaware of the impact their thoughts and emotions have on their electrical circuitry.*
>
> *Strong emotion has the power to impact on external electrical circuitry in some cases. In your case, your electrical circuitry is sensitive - extra sensitive - to your thoughts and emotions and the veil or fabric between these*

circuitries - between your thoughts and emotions and your electrical circuitry - is finer than most, so the impact of thoughts and emotions is more transitional. Mmm...is conducted more profoundly. The connectivity layer of all electrical circuitries has no shield between them in your case. One of your gifts is your ability to impact electrical circuitry with your thoughts. At the moment, this gift is unharnessed. With practice you will learn how to harness and constructively use the conductivity of the electrical circuitry both within and without.

What this is illuminating for you is the interconnectedness of all - there is no separation. The fabric between thought, intention and emotions in the human condition is fragile, or thin, and you impact on your electrical world more dynamically than most.

This is another opportunity to explore the dynamics of human thought and emotion on the electrical circuitry which has blossomed on earth today. Does this answer your question?

Cathie: Yes, thank you. Can I expand on it a little? What are the practices that I could undertake to learn how to harness that electrical energy?

TGO: We see that you write your journal. Record specifically the incidents where you are aware of your human electrical circuitry impacting on the outer electrical circuitry. Note your thoughts and emotions and intentions around the time you observe the shifts. Observe the patterns which trigger the electrical influence. That is one way.

Another is to develop a discipline of practicing illuminating small light globes by holding them in your fingers, and practice strengthening your electrical connectivity to illuminate the light globe. You will need to harness your electricity in a way that does not detract from any requirements of your body. Experiment with this. Your intuition will also be enhanced through the experimentation with electrical conductivity within the human body. You will intuitively receive how to experiment with this project.

Cathie: When I learn how to harness electricity effectively, will I be able to boost my personal energy?

TGO: Yes. It will also give you the skills and the tools to manage your energy in different circumstances where at times you will need more energy and at other times it is inappropriate to have such a flow.

In rest and relaxation times, you want your electrical system to be minimised, allow your body to rest. So you will need to experiment with a manner to increase and decrease your exposure to the electrical circuitry. This will enhance all aspects of your exploration into what is beyond the human condition.

Cathie: Thank you. Are there ways that people who don't have problems with electricity can boost their energy on a daily practice?

TGO: Yes. Everything is vibration. Connectivity to the vibration flows through the filters as unique and individual as every human being. The ability to connect to the electrical circuitry however, is not limited by these filters.

You will find intention is the most powerful resource for connecting directly with the electrical circuitry both internally and externally. This is for all.

> *It is about developing a way of harnessing this unseen phenomenon and using it constructively for upliftment and empowerment. It is a way of being "in flow" with all that is.*
>
> *Cathie: And that will be different for every person?*
>
> *TGO: Yes.*
>
> *Cathie: So it is their responsibility to find out what gives them their own flow?*
>
> *TGO: Yes.*

The information given in this session was unexpected, and intriguing. Before this session I had not thought about people as electrical circuits affected by thoughts and emotions, or realised that meditation was a way of controlling electrical flow and therefore energy levels. I thought meditation was a way to calm down, chill out.

The idea of lighting a globe in my fingers as a way of bringing my energy levels up was seductive. I found out that it is better to practice in the morning because when I got better at it, if I practiced late at night I was "buzzing" after the meditation and couldn't sleep. I practiced for at least an hour daily with a light globe and a torch for a month before the torch flickered to life (I still can't light the globe).

It gave me such a fright when the torch lit up that first time. It happened several times over the following month, but was frustratingly unresponsive most of the time. I was still skeptical, and decided after each successful session that I had imagined it, or the torch connection switch was faulty. But I gradually felt the "doorway", and when I stepped into the space where the electricity ran freely. The torch seemed to light up only when I was in that "vibration".

I continued with the channelling sessions with Julie, but I felt frustrated that there was so much to ask, and so much to ask on the answers given that I did not cover half the topics I wanted. I despaired at my fumbling inarticulate attempts and felt inadequate to the task of asking important questions. I didn't want to ask mundane questions I should work out myself.

The sessions and the information felt slightly surreal - I was still not quite believing channelling was really a "thing", but at the same time feeling the truth of the answers resonate within me. I felt like I was scratching the surface of the questions that should be asked - and that a shovel would not help me. I wanted both to dig in, and contrarily cover over and polish off the scratches like they had never been made. I felt the sessions were too bizarre to take seriously. And too important not to take very seriously.

I was torn between skepticism and awe. But mostly, I think I was in a low grade state of shock and denial. Not unlike my feelings following the lightning balls.

But the fact is that there is a lot about us and our world that we don't understand or know. Scientists can still not explain lightning. Even water is mysterious, and lightning usually comes from incredibly heavy volumes of water just hanging somehow in the sky. But as clouds generate thunder and lightning, water must have an enormous capacity for producing energy that is not properly understood.

Water is the filter through which we see, feel, hear, taste, and smell, so perhaps it is the transport vehicle that enables us to experience consciousness. Every process in our bodies requires water to facilitate it. There is something about the role of water in our lives that we take for granted, or we have overlooked, because water behaves differently to almost every other substance on earth - it has a memory, and forms structures that transmit both energy and information.

The Ripple Effect of Being:

Masaru Emoto is famous for proposing that human consciousness has an effect on the molecular structure of water. Experiments by Buckminster Fuller with the vibration of sound waves showed distinct patterns for musical notes, similar to the patterns discovered by Masaru Emoto for thought crystals in water. And water batteries were abandoned nearly three hundred years ago because of their inherently explosive nature.

If we are electrical circuits and our bodies are mostly water, I wonder why we are unaware of how powerful our untapped thoughts, intentions and language are. Perhaps the water within us provides the vehicle for the Ripple Effect of our Being. Can we dive in, to find our inner song?

8

Music and Colour

----

*There is a precise shape of emotion, and a sound
that when played, "creates" that emotion.*
Dr Manfred Clynes

I am not a mathematician. Or an artist. But I find beauty in how things come together. In particular, I love the way we can create music or art or dance so exquisitely that our emotions are engaged - that just looking at something or hearing the notes meld inside my own body creates something else. Just for that moment, the artists and I are connected. And all I can do, sitting in my little bubble of artistic incompetence, is cry with the joy of it.

Music is like a magical creation that can relax and soothe us, or enliven us and make us want to dance, or evoke emotions such as joy or sadness. Access to memories, emotions and movement is enhanced through listening to music or familiar songs. The impact music makes on us is a mystery.

At the heart of music is a mathematical coherence incorporating structure, rhythm, beat, timing, harmony, resonance and style. So much information is contained in music that a song can be identified within the first couple of bars, and the words will come to your lips without thought.

We can also be identified within a second by the way we look, talk, walk or laugh. We have our own distinct personal vibration. If we could play our own individual song, what key would we play in? The patterns we form may be created by our "key" melding with the "keys" of those around us - connecting our own natural resonance. Whenever we interact with others, there are discords, harmonies, allegro, staccato, and movements where the instruments we are diverge, converge, harmonise, conflict, play solo, or wait patiently for their cue.

Musical scales are mathematical. A scale of seven notes actually "contains" twelve notes because there are natural intervals which form depending on the key in which we play. This means that even if someone is the same soul colour as you, there may be some dissonance in the relationship because they play in a different key.

These intervals mean there are soul colours which have strong elements of two soul colours, such as a green-blue soul who is excellent at research *and* presenting their findings, or a red-orange soul who is an innovative structural engineer. The personalities and ego-dragon colours also have these sharps and flats.

In the ancient Middle East, the twelve astrological signs were given colours and identifying traits. These correlate remarkably accurately with Australian Aboriginal astrological mythology. I was surprised at how ancient philosophies, astrology, vibration and colour "fitted" together eloquently across cultures in different parts of the world.

If you have ever had your astrological chart done professionally with your time and place of birth, you may be fascinated at the level of detail and accuracy. It is like we have a place in our world influenced by where and when we took our first breath.

Certain star signs resonate together, predicting the best marriages or friends, or indicating potential clashes, and perhaps soul colours reflect similar patterns. People we "click" with are in harmony with our dimensional soul colours (soul, outward personality, inward personality and ego). Like we are "in tune".

When we are "in love" or "in tune" with someone, we are more likely to agree with them and accept behaviour even if it is contrary to our own ethical belief system. People we dislike, we will disagree with - even if their views closely match our own. Someone we are annoyed with will annoy us in ways which become almost fractal in depth and repetition, curling around our lives in endlessly repeating patterns.

Rainbows appear with specific atmospheric conditions in time and space. There has to be both sunshine and water for us to see the layers of colours in a rainbow. This experiment is about creating the "atmospheric" conditions to "see" the colours within people, starting with getting to understand why we think and feel as we do, deep inside.

Vibrations are are only heard if there is a receptor. There are vibrations around us constantly which we can only hear or see if we tune our radios and televisions into the right band-wave. Like using those instruments, we are only aware of what we tune into. It occurs to me that waves, whether they are ripples on water, electromagnetic, light or sound form patterns which are obvious when you know what you are looking at. I wonder if these are like the patterns of our consciousness.

Catching our thoughts is like learning to catch a ball. At first it slips through our fingers, or we spend a lot of time chasing it. But when we become adept at handling the ball we can direct it anywhere with precision, timing and elegance.

Practicing the thought experiment skills in this book is like practicing any new skill. We invest time and effort, trusting that each moment we spend will be an incremental step toward mastery. This requires attention, intention and repetition.

If the new skill we want to acquire is playing a musical instrument, as we learn to hone that skill beautifully our awareness grows to include the melody, harmonies, timing, rhythm, and interactions with other instruments until we can finally play our part in a song - or a symphony.

When we understand ourselves and those around us in terms of this colour model, we can learn to sing our own song beautifully, find joy in the harmonies and respect the fact that all the other instruments are required for a balanced, dynamic orchestra.

The thought experiment proposed in this book requires practice as if we are part of an orchestra. It is a method of thought designed to help us understand our complex natures and emotions. This experiment offers a baby step toward learning how to develop a bridge of communication between our bodies, our thoughts and our emotions to identify our inner song and allow our true colours to shine.

Selecting our thoughts is like selecting music. We can be fearful or angry, clinging to our ego-dragons, or we can choose to resolve our emotions by understanding our soul consciousness and with practice, this may be done as easily as choosing dance music over depressing songs.

When we come to understand the dimensions of colour we are, we can mindfully choose to be inspired by those things which bring us joy, to love the Ripple Effect of our Being, and to play our inner song with honesty and intent.

9

The Thought Experiment

Psychosophy: Wisdom of the Soul

When I first heard about the thought experiment known as Schrodinger's Cat I was, frankly, appalled. My initial reaction was that even thinking about putting a cat in a potentially fatal position is not caring, and the cat is not likely to live a long happy life whether the box is opened or not. The intention of the experiment was to change perspectives on quantum mechanics thinking about how a particle can spin clockwise and anti-clockwise at the same time. Which is a perspective anyhow - looking down on it, the spin will be in the opposite direction to looking up at it. Obviously.

The thought experiment proposed in this book can be described as an experiment about how we choose to think, and how our souls colour our thoughts. People don't have just two perspectives. We are not black or white. And we are all equally unique, so we don't have to look down on or up at anyone else.

Experiments require instigating a change to see what difference it makes to the status quo. In life, however, there is no "control" with which to compare the outcome - the act of experimenting changes the status quo. This thought experiment cannot be set up either. It is a moment by moment attempt to "snapshot" a feeling and locate its resonance in your body so the language of the soul colours can be learned.

The following experiment is a way to start practicing with your internal thought patterns:

Imagine seven mobile phones in the colours of the rainbow.

Imagine they are placed in your energy chakras - the red phone in the red chakra, the orange in the orange chakra and so on.

Each phone goes with you everywhere.

Imagine another phone in your hand. Call this phone "Consciousness". The phone in your hand can be in a negative or positive "mood" at any moment, and can dial any one of the coloured chakra phones and allow you to ask questions:

"OK, tell me: What just happened? Why? Was that my soul speaking or my ego-dragon? How could I choose to respond?"

Let's take an easy example: you have a headache. When you recognise the pain in your head, you may decide to investigate the reason, so your consciousness phone dials the red phone. Red may answer:

"Seriously, after what you drank last night can you expect me not to let you know we are hung-over and dehydrated? All our organs are flat out trying to rebalance us. If you are going to try to dull emotional pain with alcohol, you have to accept the consequences. All our networks are shorting out. Lie down, drink some water, feed us with nourishing food when we can stomach it, and think about how you are going to take better care of us in the future. And next time you are upset, lets work together to help make some better choices."

Or it may say:

"Maybe you should talk to the orange phone - its been ringing you all morning and you haven't picked up yet. It is very upset and wants to sort out some emotional issues."

Or even:

"Oh! Hi Consciousness. I think the yellow phone has been trying to get your attention for the last hour. It's making our head pound. Its yelling for some exercise to get the endorphins going and we all need some fresh air. Can you call the yellow phone to find out what's going on?"

Let's take a look at a less flippant scenario:

You are having a really bad day, and everything seems to be going wrong. The kids were grizzly and uncooperative and you were at breaking point by the time they were ready for school, you finally got them in the car, and found the car has a flat tyre. Changing it means you are hot, sweaty and dirty as well as getting the kids to school late and being late for work yourself. Your boss is in a bad mood - made worse by what he calls your "attitude" (dishevelled, stressed and panicking about unrealistic deadlines you can't meet, worried about a family member who is undergoing medical tests, and you have a hollow feeling in the pit of your stomach that your husband was home late for reasons other than unexpected overtime).

When things go wrong, they can go overwhelmingly wrong, and you may feel completely powerless to change them.

What if you realise you have access to the psychosophy phones? What if you can talk with your soul colours to discuss it all?

I don't mean obsessively brood on your anger, frustration and fear until it consumes your thoughts. I don't mean gossip about how annoying the kids are or how mean your boss can be.

I mean open the doors inside, explore your feelings and the deep reasons behind them. Just as a key has to be turned around in the lock before the door can open, it may be as simple as a flip in perspective.

Lets start with communicating feelings:

You: "Help me orange phone, I'm being overwhelmed by a tidal wave of emotion, and I'm about to start crying."

Orange phone: "No wonder honey, it's been a tough day. The kids picked up on our fear immediately this morning, and got scared themselves, so they went into panic mode and their little ego-dragons started flaring at us. Johnny got stubborn (of course - he's green), Billie got noisy and demanding (what blue doesn't when they are stressed?), and dear Zoe (our sensitive little Indigo) got clumsy and teary. Yelling at her for spilling the cereal increased her fright, and we felt angrier because we felt guilty about making her cry. We know they are calmer and happier when we are calm and loving. It's hard to be that way when so much is happening though, isn't it? Have you talked to the red phone yet? Do that and get back to me. We've got lots to go through." (Orange phones, being the emotional centre, are the gateway to heaps of information about how we feel, and very chatty and supportive!)

Red phone: "Just letting you know, our period just started. The hormone build-up has peaked, and our level of angst will start to drop, so cry if you need to, and expect the cramps to kick in any minute. A warm wheat pack will help, and a cup of tea will be soothing. Don't worry, it'll be over in a few days. We've done this before, we can do it again. No biggie, just not great timing for us with everything else that is going on. By the way, I think the Blue Phone is trying to get through to you."

Blue phone: "There's a lump in our throat blocking our connection. We need some time to practice how best to say what will come out of discussions with the orange phone, to ensure we don't let our outward personality get all dusty in the conversations we need to have with those we love. I know it's going to be difficult clearing the lump so we can connect better and sing our truth, but that is what emotions are for - working through them so we can then express them eloquently. You are doing a great job. This tough time will pass. Please don't block me out, I'm here to help. Remember, anger is our ego clinging to the past and fear is our ego clinging to the future. We can respond to the present at a different level if we clear away those cling-ons." (Blue phones can talk a lot.)

Violet phone: "While we are talking about clearing away, my love, we have way too much on our plates. Can we work out some strategies to simplify life? Can we clear the decks, identify some priorities, drop the activities that are extraneous to our purpose, our inner song? Can we stop procrastinating about the things that we need to do? We will feel much less stressed, and then we can 'do and be' in joy. Just saying."

Red phone: "I agree. I'm getting really tired, the stress hormones are at meltdown level and you seem unaware that taking paracetamol just turns you deaf to me - and I'm still hurting here even if you can't see or hear me! Don't let this little red ego-dragon take over or we will all burn out. Please help me help you. I'm only telling you things you can respond to pretty easily. We have a responsibility to work together and abdicating isn't helping. If I shut down because I feel uncared for, we're all in big trouble. We don't want to get sick. Our number one priority is: remember to breathe. When we have enough oxygen, we work better. Let's start there. Nice deep breaths so we can sing in tune. That's right. Thank you."

Green phone: "Oh that's better my dear, our heart is calmer, our rhythm sustainable. We can start to connect inside and out with compassion and understanding. Well done."

Yellow phone: "Easier for me, too, thank you. Now we can start to get some strategies in place to meet our deadlines, get our timing right.

Use our amazing ability to think clearly. Because the way that ego-dragon was flaring, our vivacious little inward personality was about to break open into messy antagonism."

Indigo phone: "Coming together with awareness takes dedicated effort, but it is worth it. We are feeling much better than five minutes ago aren't we? There are still some tough conversations and emotions to work through, and they are important, so we need true insight into our problems. Then we can be authentic in how we respond. We can cope with whatever the future holds. Hey guys, this is great. Working together, we can consciously create ripples for a harmonious future."

Our internal phones can be just as demanding as the other phones in our lives, can't they?

But this is who we are - our emotions, thoughts and actions become the states of being that create and express our personality. When we feel, observe, reflect upon and then act with clarity, our personality crystallises and establishes a platform for our future interactions with others.

We can then choose to respond with mindfulness and integrity. We can choose how our energy flows: from fear or love; draining or expanding.

Once a conversation has been initiated, it is possible to dive further into emotions which are draining you.

For example, if you identify suspicion of your partner's fidelity in your relationship, you can find out if it stems from a deep seated yellow ego-dragon fear of abandonment, or an orange inward personality in suspicious and messy overdrive, or a blue outward personality accumulating a controlling dust, or if it is based on green soul observation. The conversation about your feelings with your partner will be totally different if you have established that the emotions do not arise from your ego or personalities.

Conflicts with bosses or co-workers can be examined in the same way. Being able to eliminate - or change the polarity - of ego and personalities leaves you free to access soul honesty. This may be as simple as recognising the qualities of your boss as belonging to different soul colours to yours. You are then able to work together knowing the difference is an important additional perspective rather than a problem. So long as dragons are not poked awake.

Practicing this thought experiment enables the development of awareness, and will create change. We can learn how to choose patterns which make us feel happier when we understand the languages of our soul colours. It is a strategy for understanding others, and harmonising our internal and external worlds.

Everything we think, say and do can resonate with a clarity that rings true, feels amazing and commands respect - for yourself and those who meet you, face to face, on this platform of consciousness.

The Ripple Effect of Being will change the world within and around you.

Printed in the United States
By Bookmasters